Editor
Erica N. Russikoff, M.A.

Editor in Chief
Karen J. Goldfluss, M.S. Ed.

Cover Artist
Tony Carrillo
Brenda DiAntonis

Imaging
James Edward Grace
Craig Gunnell

Publisher
Mary D. Smith, M.S. Ed.

Author
Robert W. Smith

Teacher Created Resources
12621 Western Avenue
Garden Grove, CA 92841
www.teachercreated.com
ISBN: 978-1-4206-5036-5

Reprinted, 2026
Made in U.S.A.

Teacher Created Resources

Table of Contents

Table of Contents *(cont.)*

Introduction

The primary goal of any reading task is comprehension. *Daily Warm-Ups: Nonfiction Reading* uses high-interest, grade-level appropriate nonfiction passages followed by assessment practice to help develop confident readers who can demonstrate their skills on standardized tests. Each passage is a high-interest nonfiction text that fits one of the five topic areas: Interesting Places and Events, Scientifically Speaking, From the Past, Did You Know?, and Fascinating People. Each of these five topic areas has 30 passages, for a total of 150 passages. Each passage, as well as its corresponding multiple-choice assessment questions, is provided on one page.

Comprehension Questions

The questions in *Daily Warm-Ups: Nonfiction Reading* assess all levels of comprehension, from basic recall to critical thinking. The questions are based on fundamental reading skills found in scope-and-sequence charts across the nation:

- recall information
- use prior knowledge
- visualize
- recognize the main idea
- identify supporting details
- understand cause and effect
- sequence in chronological order
- identify synonyms and antonyms
- know grade-level vocabulary
- use context clues to understand new words
- make inferences
- draw conclusions

Readability

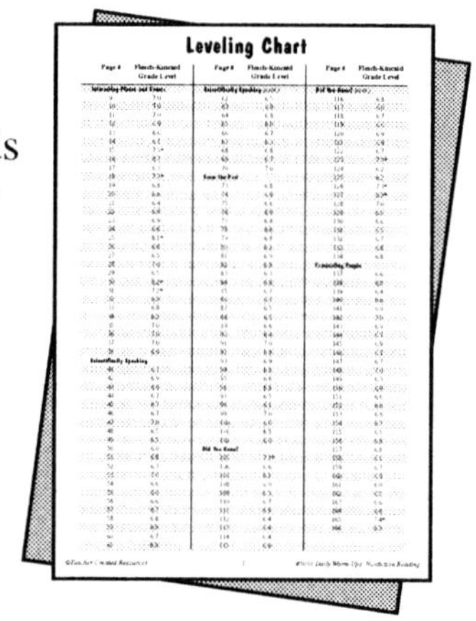
Leveling Chart

The texts have a 6.0–7.0 grade level based on the Flesch-Kincaid Readability Formula. This formula, built into Microsoft Word®, determines readability by calculating the number of words, syllables, and sentences. Multisyllabic words tend to skew the grade level, making it appear higher than it actually is. Refer to the Leveling Chart on page 175 for the approximate grade level of each passage.

In some cases, there are words necessary to a passage that increase its grade level. In those cases, the passage's grade level is followed by an asterisk in the chart. This means that in determining the grade level, the difficult words were factored in, resulting in the increased level shown before the asterisk. Upon the removal of these words, the passage received a grade level within the appropriate range. For example, in the passage, "The Liberty Bell," the grade level is 7.3. This is because the word *Pennsylvania* is repeated several times. Once the word is removed, the grade level is within range.

Including Standards and Benchmarks

The passages and comprehension questions throughout this book correlate with McREL (Mid-Continent Research for Education and Learning) Standards. Known as a "Compendium of Standards and Benchmarks," this resource is well researched. It includes standards and benchmarks that represent a consolidation of national and state standards in several content areas for grades K–12. (See page 6 for the specific McREL Standards and Benchmarks that correspond with this book.) These standards have been aligned to the Common Core State Standards. To view them, please visit *http://www.teachercreated.com/standards/*.

Introduction *(cont.)*

Practice First to Build Familiarity

Initial group practice is essential. Read aloud the first passage in each of the five topic areas and do its related questions with the whole class. Depending upon the needs of your class, you may choose to do the first three passages in each topic area as a whole class. Some teachers like to use five days in a row to model the reading and question-answering process at the start of the year. Model pre-reading the questions, reading the text, highlighting information that refers to the comprehension questions, and eliminating answers that are obviously incorrect. You may also want to model referring back to the text to ensure the answers selected are the best ones.

Student Practice Ideas

With *Daily Warm-Ups: Nonfiction Reading* you can choose to do whole-class or independent practice. For example, you can use the passages and questions for the following:

- warm-ups for lessons
- centers
- whole-group practice
- homework
- individual student work
- end-of-class activities

Whichever method you choose for using the book, it's a good idea to practice as a class how to read a passage and respond to the comprehension questions. In this way, you can demonstrate your own thought processes by "thinking aloud" to figure out an answer. Essentially, this means that you tell your students your thoughts as they come to you.

Self-Monitoring Reading Strategies

Use the reading strategies on page 174 with your students so they can monitor their own reading comprehension. Copy and distribute this page to your students, or turn it into a class poster. Have your students use these steps for this text, as well as future texts.

Record Keeping

In the sun image at the bottom, right-hand corner of each warm-up page, there is a place for you (or for students) to write the number of questions answered correctly. This will give consistency to scored pages. Use the Tracking Sheet on page 176 to record which warm-up exercises you have given to your students. Or distribute copies of the sheet for students to keep their own records.

How to Make the Most of This Book

- Read each lesson ahead of time before you use it with the class so that you are familiar with it. This will make it easier to answer students' questions.
- Set aside ten to twelve minutes at a specific time daily to incorporate *Daily Warm-Ups: Nonfiction Reading* into your routine.
- Make sure the time you spend working on the materials is positive and constructive. This should be a time of practicing for success and recognizing it as it is achieved.

The passages and comprehension questions in *Daily Warm-Ups: Nonfiction Reading* are time-efficient, allowing your students to practice these skills often. The more your students practice reading and responding to content-area comprehension questions, the more confident and competent they will become.

Standards and Benchmarks

Each passage in *Daily Warm-Ups: Nonfiction Reading* meets at least one of the following standards and benchmarks, which are used with permission from McREL. Copyright 2010 McREL. Mid-continent Research for Education and Learning. 4601 DTC Boulevard, Suite 500, Denver, CO 80237. Telephone: 303-337-0990. Web site: *www.mcrel.org/standards-benchmarks.* Correlations to the Common Core State Standards can be found at *http://www.teachercreated.com/standards/.*

Uses the general skills and strategies of the reading process

- Establishes and adjusts purposes for reading
- Uses word origins and derivations to understand word meaning
- Uses a variety of strategies to extend reading vocabulary
- Uses specific strategies to clear up confusing parts of a text
- Understands specific devices an author uses to accomplish his or her purpose
- Reflects on what has been learned after reading and formulates ideas, opinions, and personal responses to texts
- Knows parts of speech and their functions

Uses skills and strategies to read a variety of informational texts

- Reads a variety of informational texts
- Summarizes and paraphrases information in texts
- Uses new information to adjust and extend personal knowledge base
- Draws conclusions and makes inferences based on explicit and implicit information in texts
- Understands the evidence used to support an assertion in informational texts

Uses a variety of strategies to extend reading vocabulary

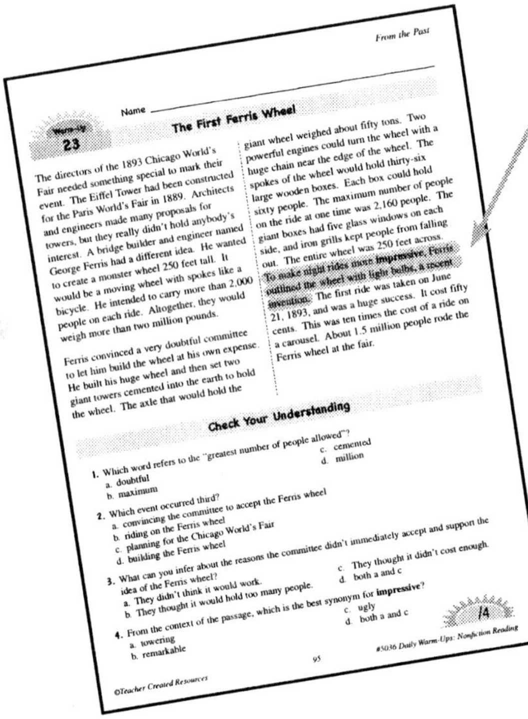

From the Past

Warm-Up 23 Name ____________

The First Ferris Wheel

The directors of the 1893 Chicago World's Fair needed something special to mark their event. The Eiffel Tower had been constructed for the Paris World's Fair in 1889. Architects and engineers made many proposals for towers, but they really didn't hold anybody's interest. A bridge builder and engineer named George Ferris had a different idea. He wanted to create a monster wheel 250 feet tall. It would be a moving wheel with spokes like a bicycle. He intended to carry more than 2,000 people on each ride. Altogether, they would weigh more than two million pounds.

Ferris convinced a very doubtful committee to let him build the wheel at his own expense. He built his huge wheel and then set two giant towers cemented into the earth to hold the wheel. The axle that would hold the giant wheel weighed about fifty tons. Two powerful engines could turn the wheel with a huge chain near the edge of the wheel. The spokes of the wheel would hold thirty-six large wooden boxes. Each box could hold sixty people. The maximum number of people on the ride at one time was 2,160 people. The giant boxes had five glass windows on each side, and iron grills kept people from falling out. The entire wheel was 250 feet across. To make night rides more **impressive**, Ferris outlined the wheel with light bulbs, a recent invention. The first ride was taken on June 21, 1893, and was a huge success. It cost fifty cents. This was ten times the cost of a ride on a carousel. About 1.5 million people rode the Ferris wheel at the fair.

Check Your Understanding

1. Which word refers to the "greatest number of people allowed"?
   a. doubtful
   b. maximum
   c. cemented
   d. million
2. Which event occurred third?
   a. convincing the committee to accept the Ferris wheel
   b. riding on the Ferris wheel
   c. planning for the Chicago World's Fair
   d. building the Ferris wheel
3. What can you infer about the reasons the committee didn't immediately accept and support the idea of the Ferris wheel?
   a. They didn't think it would work.
   b. They thought it would hold too many people.
   c. They thought it didn't cost enough.
   d. both a and c
4. From the context of the passage, which is the best synonym for **impressive**?
   a. towering
   b. remarkable
   c. ugly
   d. both a and c

/4

©Teacher Created Resources 95 #5036 Daily Warm-Ups: Nonfiction Reading

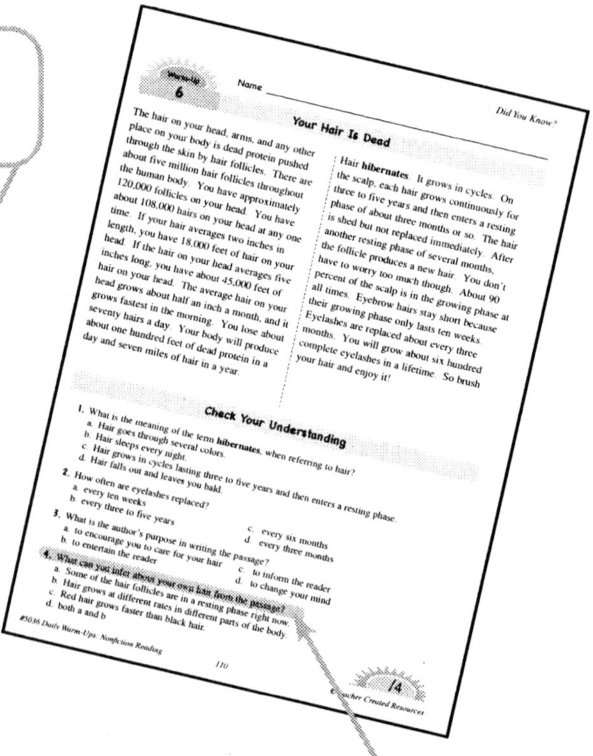

Did You Know?

Warm-Up 6 Name ____________

Your Hair Is Dead

The hair on your head, arms, and any other place on your body is dead protein pushed through the skin by hair follicles. There are about five million hair follicles throughout the human body. You have approximately 120,000 follicles on your head. You have about 108,000 hairs on your head at any one time. If your hair averages two inches in length, you have 18,000 feet of hair on your head. If the hair on your head averages five inches long, you have about 45,000 feet of hair on your head. The average hair on your head grows about half an inch a month, and it grows fastest in the morning. You lose about seventy hairs a day. Your body will produce about one hundred feet of dead protein in a day and seven miles of hair in a year.

Hair **hibernates**. It grows in cycles. On the scalp, each hair grows continuously for three to five years and then enters a resting phase of about three months or so. The hair is shed but not replaced immediately. After another resting phase of several months, the follicle produces a new hair. You don't have to worry too much though. About 90 percent of the scalp is in the growing phase at all times. Eyebrow hairs stay short because their growing phase only lasts ten weeks. Eyelashes are replaced about every three months. You will grow about six hundred complete eyelashes in a lifetime. So brush your hair and enjoy it!

Check Your Understanding

1. What is the meaning of the term **hibernates**, when referring to hair?
   a. Hair goes through several colors.
   b. Hair sleeps every night.
   c. Hair grows in cycles lasting three to five years and then enters a resting phase.
   d. Hair falls out and leaves you bald.
2. How often are eyelashes replaced?
   a. every ten weeks
   b. every three to five years
   c. every six months
   d. every three months
3. What is the author's purpose in writing the passage?
   a. to encourage you to care for your hair
   b. to entertain the reader
   c. to inform the reader
   d. to change your mind
4. What can you infer about your own hair from the passage?
   a. Some of the hair follicles are in a resting phase right now.
   b. Hair grows at different rates in different parts of the body.
   c. Red hair grows faster than black hair.
   d. both a and b

/4

#5036 Daily Warm-Ups: Nonfiction Reading 110 ©Teacher Created Resources

Draws conclusions and makes inferences based on explicit and implicit information in texts

Interesting Places and Events

Warm-Up 1

Name ______________________________

Wait Until 2061

A visitor is returning. We haven't seen this one in ages. In 2061, Halley's Comet will streak past Earth. It is named for Edmund Halley. He deduced that comets seen in 1531, 1607, and 1682 were all one in the same. He predicted its appearance in 1758. But he did not live to see it. The most ancient record of Halley's Comet comes from 1057 BCE. A Chinese book mentions it. Astronomers have noted each appearance since 239 BCE.

A comet begins as a small, icy mass far beyond Pluto in a region called the Oort Cloud. There, billions of chunks of ice water, ice ammonia, ice methane, and dust circle the solar system. Pluto's or Neptune's gravity causes the comet to start falling toward the sun. A trail of solar particles creates a visible tail of glowing gases. The tail can stretch for thirty-five million miles! The comet goes around the sun. Then it slingshots away and races once more toward the outer solar system. Most comets never return to the solar system. However, a few are short-period comets. They return at regular intervals. Halley's Comet appears every seventy-six years. Comet Encke goes by every 3.3 years.

Check Your Understanding

1. From the context of the passage, what is the meaning of a short-period comet?

a. It returns at regular intervals.
b. It is never seen but once.
c. It is made of solar particles.
d. It lasts less than a year.

2. Where do comets form?

a. near the sun
b. near Jupiter
c. in the Oort Cloud region
d. near Earth

3. Which of the following is a topic sentence?

a. Then it slingshots away and races once more toward the outer solar system.
b. A comet begins as a small, icy mass far beyond Pluto in a region called the Oort Cloud.
c. The most ancient record of Halley's Comet comes from 1057 BCE.
d. Comet Encke goes by every 3.3 years.

4. Which event occurred after Halley's death and was seen as proof that the comet returned every seventy-six years?

a. The appearance in 1984.
b. The appearance in 2061.
c. The appearance in 1057 BCE.
d. The return of the comet in 1758.

/4

Warm-Up 2

Name ______________________________

Around the World in Seventy-Two Days

When Jules Verne published his popular book, *Around the World in Eighty Days*, travel was still slow. To travel around the world in eighty days seemed impossible in the real world. In 1889, America's first female reporter, Nellie Bly, convinced her editor that she could beat that time and any man who tried to compete with her. On November 14, 1889, Nellie got on board the steamship *Augusta Victoria*, leaving Hoboken, New Jersey. The race against the clock began at 9:40 a.m.

She traveled to France where she met Jules Verne. They mapped out Nellie's **itinerary** to match the route in Jules Verne's book. Nellie went on to Italy. She then sailed through the newly dug Suez Canal. She sailed from Yemen to Ceylon (now Sri Lanka) to Singapore. There, she bought a monkey who traveled the rest of the route with her. She learned that a young female reporter had been sent by a magazine and was ahead of her. This did not stop Nellie. She continued on to Hong Kong and Japan before crossing the Pacific Ocean to San Francisco.

Nellie then traveled across the southern part of the United States by train to New Jersey. She set foot on the Jersey City train station seventy-two days, six hours, and eleven minutes after starting her journey. Her amazing race made her a national heroine.

Check Your Understanding

1. From the context of the passage, what is the meaning of **itinerary**?

a. a list of books
b. a list of destinations on a trip
c. a list of steamships
d. a list of people to meet

2. What do you think Nellie did on the trip so that people knew where she was and how she was doing?

a. She sent dispatches and articles to her newspaper to be published.
b. She sent letters to the president of the United States.
c. She gave interviews to television reporters.
d. She made telephone calls to her parents.

3. What did Nellie and Jules Verne discuss?

a. how he wrote the book
b. the route around the world
c. people to meet on the way
d. how to write a novel

4. What can you infer from the passage about the success of Nellie's competitor?

a. She didn't finish the race.
b. She quit and went home.
c. She didn't win the race.
d. She won the race.

/4

Warm-Up 3

Name ____________________

Antarctica

Antarctica is an ice-covered continent. It lies near the South Pole. It is larger than Australia and just a bit smaller than South America. Antarctica covers 5.4 million square miles. That is about 9.7 percent of Earth's land area. It is not a nation, and there are no citizens. No one lives there permanently. However, several nations have scientific research posts there.

About 98 percent of the continent is covered with ice. Its ice cap holds about 70 percent of all of the fresh water on Earth. At its thickest point, the ice covering Antarctica is about three miles in depth. The ice sheet is so thick and heavy that it keeps most of the land underwater!

Antarctica is the coldest continent on Earth. Average temperatures rarely climb over -31°F. That is still 63°F below freezing! The lowest temperature recorded on Earth was in Antarctica. It was a bone-chilling -128°F. It is also one of the driest places on the planet. There is a great deal of wind but hardly any rain or snow.

Until about eighty million years ago, Antarctica was connected to Australia. We know this because of the fossil record. Fossils of plants, reptiles, and other creatures prove that the continent was actually a tropical paradise at that time.

Check Your Understanding

1. Which continent is slightly larger than Antarctica?
- a. Australia
- b. Asia
- c. South America
- d. Greenland

2. Why do you think there are no native settlements or permanent cities on Antarctica?
- a. The climate is too cold.
- b. Food would be hard to find.
- c. There are no edible plants.
- d. all of the above

3. How do you know that Antarctica was *not* always as cold as it is today?
- a. Australia is not covered with ice.
- b. Fossil plants and animals found in Antarctica are from warmer climates.
- c. People are living on Antarctica today.
- d. Antarctica looks like it will warm up.

4. How many degrees below freezing was the lowest recorded temperature on Antarctica?
- a. -128°F
- b. -160°F
- c. -96°F
- d. -200°F

/4

Warm-Up 4

Name ______________________________

The Taj Mahal

The Taj Mahal is on the list of the Seven Wonders of the Modern World. Historians, tourists, and students of **architecture** and design admire it for two reasons. One is for its beauty. The other is the love story that led to its creation.

The Taj Mahal stands on the banks of the Yamuna River in Agra, India. Its construction began in 1631 and was finished in 1653. It is an Islamic tomb built of white marble, which was imported from all over India and neighboring lands. Its creation required the use of more than 1,000 elephants to transport the marble. More than 22,000 builders labored for twenty-one years to erect it. They used twenty-eight different kinds of precious and semi-precious stones to decorate the temple.

This "Crown Palace" is a monument to love. Shah Jahan was the fifth Mughal emperor of India. When he was a fourteen-year-old prince, he fell in love with a fifteen-year-old Persian princess. Five years later, she became his third wife. This was in 1612. He called her "Mumtaz Mahal," which means "Jewel of the Palace." They had a happy marriage. However, she died giving birth to their fourteenth child. Heartbroken, her husband ordered the building of the Taj Mahal. This tomb is a tribute to her. It still stands as an enduring symbol of their love.

Check Your Understanding

1. How old was the princess when they were married?
- a. thirty-one years old
- b. twenty years old
- c. twenty-five years old
- d. fourteen years old

2. Which culture does the Taj Mahal represent?
- a. American
- b. Islamic
- c. Jewish
- d. Chinese

3. Which of the following ideas can you infer from the passage?
- a. Mahal means "palace."
- b. White marble was valued highly in Indian buildings.
- c. The Taj Mahal is both a tomb and a temple.
- d. all of the above

4. What does **architecture** refer to?
- a. the design of buildings
- b. Indian religions
- c. the damming of rivers
- d. all of the above

/4

Warm-Up **5**

Name ______________________________

Dinosaur Provincial Park

Would you like to visit a park entirely dedicated to dinosaurs? Then you should go to Dinosaur Provincial Park. For dinosaur enthusiasts, it is the park to visit. It is in Alberta, Canada.

In 1884, a scientist went searching for coal and oil deposits. This was in the mostly unexplored lands of western Canada. He found a huge dinosaur skull along the Red Deer River. Scientists realized it was a new dinosaur. They called it the Albertosaurus. Why? It was found near the city of Alberta.

Explorers and scientists soon discovered that the area was a **treasure-trove** of dinosaur remains. A mixture of mud, sand, and minerals had perfectly preserved them. More than 150 complete dinosaur skeletons have been found there. Thousands of individual bones have been uncovered, too.

In 1955, the Canadian government created Dinosaur Provincial Park. This was done to display many of the skeletons and protect the remaining bones. In some parts of the park, scientists still search for bones. Visitors are not allowed to search for bones and remove them.

The park has displays of many dinosaurs, including the Styracosaurus. Its name means "spiked lizard." It was an eighteen-foot-long, six-foot-high horned species. It weighed 600 pounds. The Albertosaurus was thirty feet long and weighed 4,000 pounds. It walked on two legs.

Check Your Understanding

1. From the context of the passage, what is the best meaning of **treasure-trove**?

a. hidden treasure
b. gold deposits
c. worthless junk
d. a dinosaur skull

2. From your prior knowledge of dinosaurs and the context of the passage, which well-known dinosaur appears to be a close relative of the Albertosaurus?

a. Brontosaurus
b. Tyrannosaurus rex
c. Iguanodon
d. Triceratops

3. Which word refers to a mixture of mud, sand, and minerals?

a. dinosaur
b. sediment
c. riverbed
d. specimen

4. Where is Dinosaur Provincial Park located?

a. Mexico
b. the United States
c. Canada
d. California

/4

Warm-Up 6

Name ______________________________

Deer Cave, Malaysia

You probably wouldn't want to visit Deer Cave in Malaysia. The cave is massive—so massive that it can hold more people than the largest football stadium on Earth. However, millions of bats live inside. Each night as dusk falls, hundreds of thousands of bats from twelve different species fly out. They use echolocation to find and devour insects in the Malaysian rain forest. Each bat eats about one-third of an ounce of insects. Altogether, the bats eat about sixteen tons of insects every night! After the bugs are digested, the bats produce about five tons of fresh guano. That's the name for bat waste.

The guano falls to the cave floor. It is the largest pile of bat dung in the world. This dung supplies food to tens of millions of cockroaches, flies, worms, centipedes, and millipedes. The dung is rich in nutrients. That's why Deer Cave has the biggest population of cockroaches on Earth. There are so many roaches that the cave floor looks like a moving river of roaches. For this reason alone, Deer Cave is not likely to become a tourist attraction any time soon. However, the roaches and other small creatures provide food for millions of spiders, scorpions, and snakes.

Check Your Understanding

1. From the context of the passage, which of the following means the same as "guano"?
   a. dung
   b. manure
   c. waste
   d. all of the above

2. What do bats eat?
   a. insects
   b. flowers
   c. guano
   d. snakes

3. Which of the following is an opinion and *not* a fact?
   a. Bats eat one-third of an ounce of insects every night.
   b. Bats produce guano.
   c. Bats are interesting creatures.
   d. Bats hunt at night.

4. What can you infer from the passage?
   a. Bats have lived in Deer Cave for a long time.
   b. Bats hatch from eggs.
   c. People would be comfortable spending time in Deer Cave.
   d. both a and c

/4

Warm-Up 7

Name ______________________________

Niagara Falls

Niagara Falls is one of the world's most famous waterfalls. It forms part of the border between the United States and Canada. Water in the thirty-five-mile-long Niagara River flows east from Lake Erie. It goes over Niagara Falls. Then it goes into Lake Ontario.

Actually, Niagara Falls is two sets of falls. Goat Island lies between them. American Falls is about 1,060 feet long and 170 feet high. Horseshoe Falls is about 2,600 feet long and 176 feet high. Horseshoe Falls is named for its shape. It carries about nine times more water than American Falls. The thunder of the falling water can be heard more than twenty miles away. When the sun shines on the ever-present mist rising from the water, a rainbow glitters in the air.

Niagara Falls is a popular destination for tourists and honeymooners. Over the years, it has drawn plenty of daredevils, too. An American teacher was the first person to go over Niagara Falls in a barrel. In 1901, Annie Taylor was sealed into a barrel and dropped into the Niagara River. She was swept over Horseshoe Falls. When the barrel was retrieved near the base of Niagara Falls, she was alive but battered and bloody. Others who have tried the same stunt have been badly injured or killed. Often, a daredevil's vessel smashes on the rocks at the bottom. Now anyone who tries such a feat is arrested.

Check Your Understanding

1. Which of the following is an opinion and *not* a fact?
   a. second paragraph, first sentence
   b. second paragraph, last sentence
   c. first paragraph, last sentence
   d. none of the above

2. What is the author's attitude toward anyone going over Niagara Falls in a barrel?
   a. admiration
   b. humor
   c. disapproval
   d. encouragement

3. Which of these titles would best express the main idea of the passage?
   a. "American Falls"
   b. "Be Careful!"
   c. "Two Sets of Falls"
   d. "Daredevils Are Dangerous"

4. From the context of the passage, which elements are necessary to create rainbows?
   a. fine droplets of water in the air
   b. sunlight
   c. snow
   d. both a and b

/4

Warm-Up 8

Name ______________________________

Krakatoa

One of the most powerful volcanic explosions in human history occurred in 1883. It happened on the island of Krakatoa near Java. This is in Indonesia. On August 27, after half a million years of inactivity, Krakatoa awoke with a roar. Three volcanic mountains on the uninhabited island exploded. The massive blast sent a cloud of ash, dust, steam, and volcanic debris fifty miles high into the atmosphere.

More explosions and violent earthquakes occurred. The explosive force created winds that circled the globe seven times. But the worst was yet to come. The explosion caused giant waves called **tsunamis**. They roared across the water and blasted the shores of nearby islands. Just one of these waves killed 10,000 people on a neighboring island thirty miles away. At least 36,000 people were killed altogether.

Ships that were far from shore were safe from these waves. But near the coast, the waves picked up boats and threw them onto the land. Waves from the volcanic eruption and earthquake were felt as far away as the English Channel. Tsunamis were recorded in South America, too.

A tremendous noise occurred when three-quarters of the island collapsed into the sea. (It was an island about the size of New York's Manhattan Island.) The sound was so loud that people heard it 3,000 miles away. The people in Texas who heard the explosion thought it was gunfire. They were shocked to learn that it came from half a world away.

Check Your Understanding

1. Which event occurred second in the sequence of events at Krakatoa?
   a. Three-quarters of the island collapsed into the sea.
   b. Tsunamis hit neighboring islands.
   c. Three volcanic mountains exploded on Krakatoa.
   d. A cloud of debris blasted into the atmosphere.

2. Which of the following is a topic sentence?
   a. paragraph one, first sentence
   b. paragraph two, last sentence
   c. paragraph one, last sentence
   d. paragraph three, last sentence

3. From the context of the passage, what are **tsunamis**?
   a. giant earthquakes
   b. giant ocean waves
   c. giant waves of sound
   d. giant waves of lava

4. Which of these is the best summary of the entire passage?
   a. An earthquake occurred on Krakatoa, putting many lives and homes at risk.
   b. A violent volcanic eruption combined with earthquakes destroyed the island of Krakatoa and caused enormous damage.
   c. Waves of sound could be heard thousands of miles away.
   d. Tsunamis are giant waves that cause a lot of damage.

/4

Name ____________________

Warm-Up 9

Mysterious Explosion in Russia

The Tunguska River is in central Siberia, Russia. It was the site of the most mysterious explosion in world history. On June 30, 1908, a violent blast slammed into the area with the force of a hydrogen bomb. Yet this was almost forty years before such a bomb was invented. The explosion leveled thousands of square miles of forest in seconds. It was a mostly unpopulated area. However, eyewitnesses described a fiery, explosive sky, waves of intense heat, and a thunderous noise. The blast knocked cows and people right off their feet more than thirty miles away. The sound was heard more than six hundred miles away.

What caused this blast? Even now, scientists aren't sure. Several suggestions have been made. Some have suggested that a large meteorite or asteroid burst through Earth's atmosphere and exploded. But there is no **crater** in the area. Meteorites and asteroids are composed of rock and metal. It seems there would have been an impact crater.

Other scientists believe that a small asteroid exploded in the air before hitting the ground. That's why there is no crater. The event did occur at the same time that Earth was passing through the orbit of Comet Encke. The explosion could have resulted from an atmospheric collision with a large piece of the comet's tail. That would explain no crater. Still, the mystery remains. Since it happened more than one hundred years ago, will it ever be solved?

Check Your Understanding

1. How many years ago did the mysterious explosion occur?
   a. more than 1,000 years ago
   b. more than 100 years ago
   c. during a world war
   d. in 1970
2. From the context of the passage, what is a **crater**?
   a. a gigantic hole in the earth
   b. a long ditch in the ground
   c. a new lake
   d. a kind of planet
3. Which of these did *not* happen during the Tunguska event?
   a. Scientists recorded the crash during the event.
   b. A hydrogen bomb exploded.
   c. The explosion leveled thousands of square miles of trees.
   d. both a and b
4. What can you infer from the passage?
   a. Scientists are deeply divided over the cause of the explosion.
   b. Scientists don't want to know the cause of the explosion.
   c. A hydrogen bomb exploded in the region.
   d. Alien spacecraft caused the explosion.

/4

Warm-Up 10

Name ______________________________

July 4, 1826

The Declaration of Independence was made public on July 4, 1776. Two very important people helped create that document. Their names are Thomas Jefferson and John Adams. Jefferson wrote the first draft. Members of the committee, including John Adams, made changes to it. Then the Continental Congress changed it some more. At last, it was ready. It was read aloud on the steps of Independence Hall. The document lists the reasons why the colonists wanted to break free of Great Britain.

John Adams went on to serve as a **diplomat** to foreign countries. He was also vice president under George Washington. Then he became the second president of the United States. Jefferson also served as a diplomat to France. He was the governor of Virginia. He was also secretary of state under Washington and vice president under Adams. Then he became the third president of the United States.

Adams and Jefferson became political opponents during their presidential years. After retiring from public life, they restored their friendship. Both fell ill in 1826. When the 93-year-old Adams died on July 4, 1826, his last words were: "Thomas Jefferson survives." He didn't know that five hours earlier, the 83-year-old Jefferson had passed away. It seems fitting that two of the great heroes of American freedom died hours apart on the fiftieth anniversary of the United States' birth.

Check Your Understanding

1. From the context of the passage, what is the meaning of **diplomat**?
   a. a political leader
   b. a representative to a foreign country
   c. a president
   d. a businessman
2. Which job did Adams and Jefferson *not* have in common?
   a. diplomat to foreign countries
   b. president of the United States
   c. vice president of the United States
   d. governor of Virginia
3. You can infer that during their presidencies, Adams and Jefferson
   a. were less friendly and opposed each other's policies.
   b. fought in duels.
   c. regretted the Declaration of Independence.
   d. paid no attention to each other's opinions.
4. Which event occurred third?
   a. Adams made changes to the Declaration of Independence.
   b. Jefferson wrote the first draft of the Declaration of Independence.
   c. The Continental Congress made changes to the Declaration of Independence.
   d. The Declaration of Independence was publicly proclaimed.

/4

Warm-Up 11

Name ____________________

The Coastal Redwoods

Coastal redwoods grow on a narrow strip of land forty-seven miles wide. This strip lies along the Pacific Coast from the Oregon-California border south for 450 miles to Monterey Bay, California. This area receives about 100 inches of rainfall and a lot of fog every year. This supplies the moisture vital for the growth of these kinds of trees.

Redwoods developed about sixty-five million years ago. They grew in North America, Asia, and Europe, in areas where the weather was warm and wet year-round. Due to climate change, by three million years ago, only three species of redwoods survived. One is in China, one is along the California coast, and one is found in the California Sierra Nevada mountains.

Redwoods live for a very long time, most living 500 to 700 years. Some specimens are much older. The oldest known tree was 2,200 years old. In contrast, oaks may live for 400 years. Maple trees seldom reach 300 years of age.

Redwoods have thick bark. It does not burn even during wildfires. The bark contains a bitter-tasting chemical that keeps insects from eating it. Redwood roots are unusually strong and wrap around other roots. This makes the trees hard to topple even in high winds. If one falls, it will send up sprouts from its stump.

Redwoods are gigantic. The tallest known one was 378 feet high (about the height of a 38-story building)! Some trunks have a diameter of twenty-two feet or more. It would take sixty adults with outstretched arms to encircle such a tree.

Check Your Understanding

1. Which of these is *not* a reason redwoods grow and survive?
   - a. They get a great deal of moisture.
   - b. They fall easily.
   - c. They can grow again by a stump sprouting.
   - d. Their roots intertwine underground.

2. How does the bark protect redwoods?
   - a. It doesn't taste good to insects.
   - b. It attracts insects.
   - c. It does not burn easily.
   - d. both a and c

3. What can you infer about the survival of redwoods now compared to millions of years ago?
   - a. There used to be many species of redwoods.
   - b. Much of Earth was wetter millions of years ago.
   - c. Most climates don't support redwood growth.
   - d. all of the above

4. From the context of the passage, what is the likely meaning of "stump sprouting"?
   - a. the process of regrowing a tree from a stump
   - b. the process of planting a stump in water
   - c. the process of growing grass on a stump
   - d. the process of growing flowers on a stump

/4

Warm-Up 12

Name ______________________________

Ice Ages

You are living in a time between ice ages. Ice ages are periods when Earth is so cold that the polar ice caps grow huge. They can last for millions of years. Such periods have occurred at irregular intervals during the last 2.3 billion years of Earth's history. In the last one billion years alone, there have been four ice ages. One of them lasted one hundred million years.

The most recent ice age was called the Pleistocene Ice Age. It started about two million years ago. It ended just 10,000 years ago. People were alive at that time. Still, it ended about 5,000 years before complex human civilizations began. During an ice age, there are periods of extreme cold called **glacials**. Warmer periods are called interglacials. The Pleistocene Ice Age had seventeen glacials and sixteen interglacials.

The last glacial period was called the Holocene Glacial. It reached its high point about 18,000 years ago. At its height, not only were the North and South Poles covered with ice, but also much of North America, Europe, Tasmania, and New Zealand. Even Hawaii had glaciers.

An ice sheet one mile thick covered what is now London and Washington, D.C. At that time, ice covered about 40 percent of Earth's surface. Melting glaciers dug and filled the Great Lakes. The Great Salt Lake in Utah is a remnant of this last ice age, too.

Check Your Understanding

1. Which of the following was the last glacial period?
   a. the Pleistocene
   b. the Holocene
   c. the Great Lakes
   d. today

2. From the context of the passage, what is a **glacial**?
   a. an intense cold period when ice forms
   b. a warm period between ice ages
   c. a period with no ice on Earth
   d. a dinosaur period

3. What can you infer about ice ages and the development of complex human societies?
   a. Complex human societies only succeed during ice ages.
   b. Human societies lived in Washington, D.C., and London during the Holocene Glacial.
   c. Complex human societies developed more easily in warm periods of Earth's history.
   d. There were no complex human societies before the 18th century.

4. From the context of the passage, which word is an antonym for **glacial**?
   a. ice age
   b. society
   c. glacier
   d. interglacial

/4

Warm-Up 13

Name ____________________

The Grand Canyon

The Grand Canyon is one of the world's great natural wonders. It extends about 277 miles through northern Arizona. The Colorado River begins in the Rocky Mountains of northern Colorado. It flows for 1,450 miles through the base of the canyon it carved. It eventually empties into the Gulf of California, which is a part of the Pacific Ocean. It took this river billions of years to form the Grand Canyon. Slowly, it wore away the rock, exposing ancient rocks and fossil specimens. Rocks at the base are two billion years old, among the oldest found on Earth.

The Grand Canyon is more than a mile deep in some places. In width, it varies from four to eighteen miles. The top of the canyon is mostly flat. It is covered with a forest of oak, spruce, and pine trees. A few bushes and small pines cling to the walls of the cliffs. Bushes dot the canyon floor. Many different animals live in the Grand Canyon, including mountain lions, bighorn sheep, mule deer, and bobcats.

The Grand Canyon was the site of two different mountain ranges that rose and were worn away during the long period of its existence. At times, ancient seas flowed in from the oceans. The rock walls contain remains of **prehistoric** plants and animals from both land and sea. For scientists studying Earth's natural history, the Grand Canyon is a giant laboratory.

Check Your Understanding

1. Which of the following statements would *not* be relevant information about the Grand Canyon?
   a. The Grand Canyon was first explored by John Wesley Powell.
   b. The Colorado River can pick up rocks as large as cars.
   c. The Colorado River keeps digging deeper into the canyon floor.
   d. There are canyons in several states.

2. From the context of the passage, what is the best meaning of **prehistoric**?
   a. older than 200 years
   b. older than the history of man's life on Earth
   c. before 1,500 CE
   d. older than your parents

3. Which of the following sentences is a topic sentence?
   a. The Grand Canyon is one of the world's great natural wonders.
   b. The top of the canyon is mostly flat.
   c. The rock walls contain remains of prehistoric plants and animals from both land and sea.
   d. At times, ancient seas flowed in from the oceans.

4. What is the oldest age of rocks in the Grand Canyon?
   a. 4.6 billion years old
   b. two billion years old
   c. 2,000 years old
   d. 200 years old

/4

Warm-Up 14

Name ______________________________

The Metropolitan Museum of Art

The Metropolitan Museum of Art is in New York City. It is one of the world's great storehouses of art. It opened in 1870. The museum is open to the public. The idea is to let all people view great art. The original building has had many additions. The Met is twenty times larger now than when it was first built. It houses more than two million objects.

The Met's first **acquisition** was a Roman stone coffin. This type of tomb is called a **sarcophagus**. It was joined by Egyptian artifacts and objects recovered from ancient societies. There are classical Greek marble statues and parts of temples. The Met has furniture on display from the great European castles of the Middle Ages. Visitors can see more than 15,000 pieces of arms and armor. These span twenty-three centuries.

Artwork from ancient Egypt and medieval Europe grace its walls. Popular 19th century impressionists, such as Vincent Van Gogh, have a number of works on exhibit. What's the biggest painting? The canvas of "Washington Crossing the Delaware." It's over twelve feet tall and twenty-one feet wide!

You can learn more about the museum by reading *From The Mixed-Up Files of Mrs. Basil E. Frankweiler* by E. L. Konigsburg. It is a sixth-grade mystery set in the museum.

Check Your Understanding

1. From the context of the passage, what is a **sarcophagus**?
   a. a bed
   b. a stone coffin
   c. a castle
   d. a statue
2. From the context of the passage, what is the meaning of **acquisition**?
   a. something old
   b. a popular item
   c. something bought or gained
   d. a coffin
3. What is the main idea of the passage?
   a. The Met has a lot of paintings from impressionists.
   b. The Met is a great museum with many extraordinary historical and artistic treasures.
   c. The Met is in New York City.
   d. The Met has a lot of arms, armor, and furniture from castles.
4. Why was the Met originally built?
   a. to get some art out of storage places
   b. to provide a museum for rich and famous visitors
   c. to provide an art museum for ordinary people
   d. to fill up an empty lot in New York City

/4

Warm-Up 15

Name ______________________________

The Lincoln Memorial

The Lincoln Memorial is located on the National Mall. The Mall is in the heart of the nation's capitol in Washington, D.C. The exterior of this beautiful monument is made of white Colorado marble. It has thirty-six columns. They surround a central block. They stand for the thirty-six states that made up the United States at the time of Lincoln's death. The name of each of these states and its date of admission to the Union are **inscribed** at the top of the Lincoln Memorial.

There is a huge white marble statue of Abraham Lincoln. It sits on an armchair inside the chamber. It is nineteen feet high. American sculptor Daniel Chester French carved it. The statue was dedicated in 1922.

The text of the Gettysburg Address is engraved on a stone tablet. It is in the south chamber of the Lincoln Memorial. Lincoln's second inaugural address is engraved in the north chamber. Above Lincoln's head is this inscription: "In this temple, as in the hearts of the people for whom he saved the Union, the memory of Abraham Lincoln is enshrined forever."

The Lincoln Memorial is open day and night. Many people enjoy viewing it at dusk. At that time, some people say that the light makes it look as though Lincoln is watching over the nation he once loved.

Check Your Understanding

1. From the context of the passage, what is the meaning of **inscribed**?
   a. scribbled in ink
   b. written or engraved on a surface
   c. a kind of marble
   d. a stone column

2. What was Daniel Chester French's occupation?
   a. architect
   b. president
   c. sculptor
   d. painter

3. Why were the Gettysburg Address and the second inaugural address inscribed on the memorial?
   a. There were no other copies of the documents.
   b. They were written about Lincoln.
   c. They needed to fill up space.
   d. They were Lincoln's most famous speeches.

4. Which of the following facts would *not* be relevant to the passage about the Lincoln Memorial?
   a. Lincoln helped preserve the Union.
   b. Lincoln's speeches inspired Americans.
   c. The president of the Confederacy was Jefferson Davis.
   d. The Lincoln Memorial is made of marble.

/4

Warm-Up 16

Name ____________________

The Washington Monument

The Washington Monument was built to honor George Washington. He was America's first president. Its construction was discussed even before his death. Designers and public leaders proposed different designs. They helped to raise money, too. However, lack of funds and design arguments halted work on it several times. The cornerstone was laid on July 4, 1848. Construction took thirty-seven years to complete. The monument was dedicated in 1885. This was almost ninety years after Washington's death.

The monument is an obelisk. The shaft of white marble slowly tapers to a point. That's why the walls are fifteen feet thick at the base and just eighteen inches thick at the top. Its top is shaped like a pyramid.

The monument's white marble blocks came from **quarries** in Maryland and Massachusetts. They are held together with a cement-like mortar. There is no metal reinforcement. The monument weighs 90,854 tons. That's as much as 60,000 cars! The Washington Monument is the world's tallest masonry structure (stone and mortar). It is the tallest structure in the nation's capital. It will remain that way. It is against the law to build anything taller.

Eight small windows are located at the 500-foot-level. There are two windows on each side. They offer a beautiful view of the city. An elevator gives visitors a fast ride to the top.

Check Your Understanding

1. From the context of the passage, what are **quarries**?
   a. places where wine is stored
   b. places where wood is kept
   c. places where stone is dug out of the ground
   d. places where railroad cars are kept

2. What material holds the marble blocks in place?
   a. steel
   b. bricks
   c. nothing
   d. mortar

3. From the context of the passage, what natural event might pose the most danger to the Washington Monument?
   a. floods
   b. blizzards
   c. long periods of heat
   d. earthquakes

4. Which word describes the shape of the monument as a towering shaft of white marble?
   a. obelisk
   b. quarry
   c. pyramid
   d. cylinder

/4

Warm-Up 17

Name ____________________

The Appalachian Mountains

The Appalachian Mountains run through eastern North America. They extend from Newfoundland, Canada, all the way to Alabama. Four mountain ranges are included in the Appalachian system. They are the Alleghenies of New York, the White Mountains of New Hampshire, the Blue Ridge Mountains of Virginia and North Carolina, and the Great Smoky Mountains of Tennessee and North Carolina.

Geologists know that parts of the Appalachian Mountains formed from 750 million to one billion years ago. These mountains are not nearly as tall as the Rocky Mountains in the American West or the Himalaya Mountains in Asia. In fact, Mount Mitchell in North Carolina is the tallest peak. It is 6,684 feet high. That's just 25 percent as tall as Mt. Everest.

You can walk the length of the Appalachian Mountains along the Appalachian National Scenic Trail. American Indians once used its winding path. It is 2,144 miles long. The trail starts at Mount Katahdin in Maine and goes to Springer Mountain in Georgia. Along the way, hikers pass through fourteen states, eight national forests, and two national parks. Most people hike just a section of the trail. A few thru-hikers do the whole route. Hiking starts in March and ends in October.

Check Your Understanding

1. Where are the Appalachian Mountains located?
   a. the western United States
   b. in Asia near Mt. Everest
   c. in eastern North America
   d. in the center of the United States
2. Which people first made the path along the Appalachian Trail?
   a. park rangers
   b. thru-hikers
   c. lumbermen
   d. American Indians
3. Which of the following is an opinion and *not* a fact?
   a. The tallest peak is 6,684 feet high.
   b. The Great Smoky Mountains are in Tennessee.
   c. The Appalachian Mountains are the most beautiful mountains in America.
   d. Many rivers begin in the Appalachians as small streams.
4. What can you infer from reading the first paragraph?
   a. The Appalachian Mountains are new and tall.
   b. Mountain ranges are larger than mountain systems, such as the Appalachians.
   c. Mountain ranges are smaller than mountain systems, such as the Appalachians.
   d. The Appalachian Mountains have three ranges.

/4

Warm-Up 18

Name ______________________________

The Statue of Liberty

France and the United States became friends during the Revolutionary War. France made the Statue of Liberty as a gift for the United States. It celebrated the 100th anniversary of the Declaration of Independence.

Frederic Auguste Bartholdi, a French sculptor, created the Statue of Liberty. He took twelve years to build it. He based the face on his mother as a young woman. Completed in 1884, the sculpture stood on display in France for a year. Then it was taken apart. It crossed the Atlantic in 214 huge packing crates. The ship carrying the crates nearly went down in a storm.

When the sculpture arrived, it was put on a granite pedestal. It stands on the twelve-acre Liberty Island in New York. The Statue of Liberty's official name is *Liberty Enlightening the World.* Its location is close to the Ellis Island **immigrant** station. It is a symbol of America's welcome to immigrants.

The Statue of Liberty is covered with copper sheets. It weighs 225 tons. There are 354 steps to the crown. The crown has seven rays. They represent the seven seas and continents. Lady Liberty holds a tablet. Inscribed on it is the date July 4, 1776, in Roman numerals.

Check Your Understanding

1. What date is written in Roman numerals on the tablet held by Lady Liberty?
   a. January 1, 1884
   b. July 4, 1886
   c. July 4, 1776
   d. February 22, 1732

2. Which of these titles would best express the main idea of the passage?
   a. "A Statue for Washington"
   b. "Celebrating the Revolution"
   c. "The Statue of Liberty as an American Symbol"
   d. "Climbing the Statue of Liberty"

3. From the context of the passage, what is the best meaning of **immigrant**?
   a. a person who leaves a country
   b. a person who enters a country to live there
   c. a person who builds statues
   d. a tourist

4. What is the Statue of Liberty built upon?
   a. an old ship
   b. a pedestal
   c. dirt
   d. copper sheeting

/4

Warm-Up 19

Name ____________________

Angkor Wat

One thousand years ago, the largest city in the world was Angkor Thom in Cambodia. More than one million people lived in this city. No other city in the world could support this many people. Emperor Suryavarman II was the ruler of the great Khmer Empire. He controlled Angkor Thom and most of Southeast Asia. He ordered the construction of Angkor Wat, which became the largest temple in the world. The huge temple stands outside the city. It was built as a combination of a royal palace and a Hindu temple. The king lived there and was worshipped as a god-king. This unique temple was surrounded by a deep water-filled **moat**. The moat was more than 620 feet wide. Inside the walls of the temple, there were shrines and galleries. There was a central dome-shaped pyramid more than 200 feet high. Skilled artists created carvings and statues throughout the temple.

The capital city of Angkor Thom was defended both by water and warriors. The people were very dependent upon rice as their staple food. They built two huge tanks to store water. Each held more than two billion gallons of water. The water was used for watering rice and other crops. It was used for drinking, personal cleanliness, and **sanitation**. The water also filled a moat that surrounded the city. This man-made river helped defend against enemy armies. No one knows why the ancient city and temple were abandoned to the jungle sometime after 1100 CE.

Check Your Understanding

1. Which of the following is the name of a temple?
   a. Suryavarman
   b. Cambodia
   c. Angkor Thom
   d. Angkor Wat
2. From the context of the passage, what is the best meaning of **moat**?
   a. a man-made, deep ditch around a castle, temple, or city
   b. a lake in the middle of a city
   c. a small stream in front of a castle, temple, or city
   d. a pile of rocks
3. Which religion was practiced by the Khmer people?
   a. Islam
   b. Christianity
   c. Hinduism
   d. Buddhism
4. From the context of the passage, what is the meaning of **sanitation**?
   a. swimming
   b. disposal of waste
   c. personal defense
   d. water warfare

/4

Warm-Up 20

Name ______________________________

The Eiffel Tower

The Eiffel Tower was built for the 100th celebration of the French Revolution that began in 1789. The Eiffel Tower was the **focal point** of the 1889 World's Fair in Paris. Seven hundred people submitted designs. Yet all the judges chose the one done by Gustave Eiffel. Work began in 1887. It was done two years later. About 50 engineers, 100 iron workers, and 120 laborers worked on it. When it was finished, Eiffel used the tower to conduct experiments. He studied weather and flight.

The Eiffel Tower weighs about 10,000 tons. It is made of 15,000 pieces of iron. They are held together by 2.5 million rivets. It takes forty tons of paint to cover it! It is painted every seven years. The temperature affects the structure's height. It varies from 984 to 990 feet tall. (It is taller on hot days.) In addition to seven elevators, it has 1,665 steps.

The city of Paris owns the building. It serves as a radio-broadcasting tower. It is also an observation tower. It is the most-visited paid monument on Earth. Millions go there each year. On a clear day, a visitor can see about thirty-seven miles at the top. A mountain climber has scaled the Eiffel Tower. Parachutists have landed on it, too. Have you ever been to the Eiffel Tower?

Check Your Understanding

1. Which of these facts would *not* be relevant to the passage?
   a. Weather experiments included barometers and other devices.
   b. Flight experiments dealt with air and wind resistance.
   c. About 6.8 million people visit the tower each year.
   d. The French Revolution led to many deaths in France.

2. From the context of the second sentence, what is the meaning of **focal point**?
   a. an eye
   b. something that holds the eye's attention
   c. a kind of sport
   d. something you want to buy

3. From the context of the passage, what word means "all the individuals agreed"?
   a. dissent
   b. unanimous
   c. disapproved
   d. reluctant

4. From the context of the passage, what can you infer about Gustave Eiffel?
   a. Eiffel wasn't married.
   b. Eiffel didn't plan the tower very well.
   c. Eiffel was a man with very few interests.
   d. Eiffel was a man with many interests and abilities.

/4

Warm-Up 21

Name ______________________________

The World Cup

The World Cup is one of the biggest sporting events in the world. This great soccer championship features players from thirty-two nations. Each nation wants to win the cup by becoming the number one soccer team. The World Cup is a worldwide contest that takes place only once every four years. However, it holds the attention of much of the planet when the games begin. The World Cup was created in 1928, and the first World Cup games were held in Uruguay in 1930. It was an all-male contest at the time. The first women's World Cup was held in China in 1991.

Soccer is not quite as popular in the United States as basketball, football, or baseball. However, it still has millions of followers. People all over the world often get up in the middle of the night or skip work to watch their nation's team compete. More than five billion people watch the final match on television. That is most of the people living on the planet. During the contests leading up to the final game, people in the winning nations often hold street parties to celebrate their teams' **victories**.

Some countries seem to be the best in the game for a period of time. When Pele played for Brazil in 1970, his team won the World Cup. Brazil's team is considered one of the greatest. Pele is regarded as the best soccer player by many fans. Brazil has won a total of five World Cups, far more than any other nation.

Check Your Understanding

1. Who is Pele?
   - a. a coach
   - b. an average soccer player
   - c. a Brazilian team
   - d. one of the greatest soccer players
2. When was the first women's World Cup?
   - a. 1928
   - b. 1997
   - c. 1930
   - d. 1991
3. Which of the following is the best topic sentence?
   - a. paragraph one, first sentence
   - b. paragraph two, first sentence
   - c. paragraph three, first sentence
   - d. paragraph one, last sentence
4. From the context of the passage, which is the best antonym for **victories**?
   - a. wins
   - b. happiness
   - c. results
   - d. defeats

/4

Warm-Up **22** Name ____________________

Mount Rushmore

Mount Rushmore National Memorial stands in the Black Hills of South Dakota. It is a monument to four American presidents. They represent the courage and vision of a young nation. George Washington was the winning general in the American Revolution. He was also the first president. Thomas Jefferson wrote the Declaration of Independence. As president, he bought the Louisiana Territory. Abraham Lincoln guided the nation through the suffering of the Civil War. Theodore Roosevelt led the nation into its years of power in the 20th century.

The idea of a monument dedicated to the presidents was born in 1924. The sculptor who designed and led the project was Gutzon Borglum. He was the son of Danish immigrants. A respected artist, he had already worked on a mountain statue in Georgia. The Mount Rushmore project began in 1925. It was completed in 1941 just after the sculptor died. Workers carved the giant faces out of stone, using dynamite and jackhammers. The statues are sixty feet high. They are solid granite and can be found at the top of the nearly 6,000-foot-high Mount Rushmore. This is a 60 million-year-old mountain. More than 450,000 tons of rock were removed during construction. The actual work only took a little less than seven years. But there were many periods where no money was available. The actual cost was about one million dollars. Most of the cost was paid by the federal government.

Check Your Understanding

1. What was the approximate cost of the monument at Rushmore?
   a. ten million dollars
   b. one hundred million dollars
   c. one million dollars
   d. one billion dollars

2. From the context of the passage, which word refers to "a time of distress or pain"?
   a. construction
   b. nation
   c. granite
   d. suffering

3. Which American presidents are carved into Mount Rushmore?
   a. Theodore and Franklin Roosevelt
   b. John Adams and Thomas Jefferson
   c. Abraham Lincoln and Theodore Roosevelt
   d. George Washington and Franklin Roosevelt

4. Which of the following would be a good title for the passage?
   a. "A Monument for Presidents"
   b. "A North Dakota Highlight"
   c. "A Sculptor Dynamites a President"
   d. "From Famous People to a Monument"

/4

Warm-Up 23

Name ______________________

The Wall

The Wall honors 2,700,000 men and women who served in Vietnam between 1959 and 1975. It is a silent tribute to the 58,267 men and women who died during that long war. The idea for the memorial came from a wounded veteran. His name is Jan Scruggs. He was deeply concerned and unhappy. The war had caused anger and division in the United States. He wanted to make up for the poor attitude shown towards returning veterans. They were not welcomed as earlier war veterans had been. Congress approved his idea. Supporters began raising money for a memorial. The fund collected nine million dollars. The money came from individuals and community groups. No government funds were used.

Of the 1,421 designs that were submitted, Maya Lin won the national competition for her wall design. She was a college student at the time. Her parents had fled from Communist China to America. (She had received only a B- from her professor for the same design.) Her black granite wall of names was not popular right away. However, people soon recognized the beauty and simplicity of the monument. Construction began in March of 1982. It was finished in November of the same year. Later, a statue of the "Three Fighting Men" was added. This was in 1984. A flagpole flying the American flag was also added. You can visit the monument anytime. It is open seven days a week, twenty-four hours a day. Many former soldiers and family members visit it. They search for the names of loved ones carved on the wall.

Check Your Understanding

1. Who led the effort to create a memorial for Vietnam veterans?
   a. army generals
   b. Jan Scruggs
   c. Maya Lin
   d. the president of the United States

2. From the context of the passage, which of the following can you infer about the Vietnam War?
   a. Many Americans had opposed the war.
   b. Many Americans weren't very supportive of returning veterans.
   c. The war was very popular.
   d. both a and b

3. Which of the following is the best topic sentence?
   a. paragraph one, last sentence
   b. paragraph two, last sentence
   c. paragraph one, first sentence
   d. paragraph two, first sentence

4. What is the wall made of?
   a. green jade
   b. gray granite
   c. black granite
   d. black marble

/4

Warm-Up 24

Name ______________________________

The Himalayas

The Himalayan mountain range contains the highest mountains in the world. These mountains are young compared to other ranges. They began forming about 60 to 65 million years ago. By comparison, the Appalachian range is 250 to 300 million years old. **Tectonic plates**, which are huge slabs of rock on which continents sit, often bump together. They cause earthquakes and push up mountains. The tectonic plate on which India sits is pressing into the giant landmass of Eurasia. This pushes up the landmass, forming massive wrinkles. These wrinkles are the foundation of the Himalayas.

The plate is still pushing up against Asia. So the Himalayan Mountains are still growing at about one inch every five years. The land at the top of these mountains was once a part of the ocean seabed. Fossils of sea creatures are still stuck in the rocks at the top of these mountains.

Mount Everest is the tallest mountain in the world at 29,028 feet. It is in the Himalayas, as is K2 at 28,250 feet. There are six other mountains in the range over 26,500 feet. All of them are still growing. These mountains are often called the "Rooftop of the World." The word "Himalaya" comes from a word meaning "house of snow." The range stretches more than 1,500 miles through many countries in central Asia.

Check Your Understanding

1. Which two continents form the landmass of Eurasia?
- a. Africa and Asia
- b. Europe and America
- c. Asia and Europe
- d. Asia and India

2. What is a **tectonic plate**?
- a. an instrument for measuring mountains
- b. a continent-sized slab of rock
- c. an ocean
- d. a mountain

3. What is the meaning of **Himalaya**?
- a. the opposite of what might be expected
- b. ironing a continent
- c. pushing down on the earth
- d. house of snow

4. How do scientists know that the Himalayan mountaintops were once on the ocean floor?
- a. They found tectonic plates.
- b. They learned it from native legends.
- c. Ocean fossils were found on the tops of mountains.
- d. A book said they were.

/4

Warm-Up 25

Name ______________________________

Ellis Island—Gateway to America

The first United States immigration center was on Ellis Island. It was located near the Statue of Liberty in New York Harbor. The center was opened on January 1, 1892. There were more than thirty-five buildings to help people who wanted to become Americans. These included a Great Hall where more than 5,000 people a day entered the country over many years. Many of these were children. The center was very busy in its first twenty years. Then it had long periods of limited use before it was closed.

Between 1892 and 1924, more than twelve million people passed through the center. It became the doorway for many new citizens to enter the nation. However, it was also a place of tears and pain for some. People who were not wanted were not allowed to enter the country. They were sent back home. Some of them were told they had dangerous diseases. They might make others sick. Some were unable to work or care for themselves. However, fewer than 1 percent of all who came were not allowed to stay.

The center was closed in 1954. In 1990, it reopened as a museum. It honors over four hundred years of the country's immigrant history. The museum has many interesting **historic** papers and passenger lists from ships. It displays photos of many kinds of ships. There are many old pictures of people in the center. There is a great deal of information about more than twenty-five million immigrants, as well as a Wall of Honor. *Letters from Rifka* by Karen Hesse is an excellent children's book describing one young girl's efforts to get through the center and join her family.

Check Your Understanding

1. From the context of the passage, what is the best meaning of **historic**?
   a. something fresh
   b. something from the past
   c. something recent
   d. something delivered by ship

2. Which materials are housed in the Ellis Island Museum?
   a. passenger lists
   b. photos
   c. historic papers
   d. all of the above

3. Which reason(s) could be used to exclude an immigrant?
   a. having a dangerous disease
   b. being able to work
   c. having little money
   d. both a and b

4. When was the immigration center closed?
   a. 1990
   b. 1892
   c. 1954
   d. 1924

/4

Warm-Up 26

Name ____________________

The Iditarod Sled Dog Race

The Iditarod Sled Dog Race is the most popular sporting event in Alaska. It is a bridge between the past and the present in that state. It also creates a cultural bond between the American Indians and settlers from the United States. Both groups relied upon dog sleds for transportation until recent times.

The race is based upon the famous run of a sled-dog **musher** named Leonard Seppala in 1925. He made emergency deliveries of **diphtheria** serum to doctors in isolated villages. The yearly race began in 1973 with about fifty mushers, or sled-dog drivers. There are both male and female drivers and their dog-sled teams. In total, there are about 1,000 dogs. In addition to the driver, the sled carries food for the drivers and their dogs. There is also a radio for communication, as well as lamps. Extra booties are brought to protect the dogs' feet. Some sled parts and tools are carried for emergency repairs. Sometimes, even an extra lightweight sled is brought along for the final leg of the journey.

There are two routes used on different years. This protects the environment. The Northern Route is 1,112 miles long. It is used one year. The Southern Route is 1,131 miles long and used the next year. The official length of the race is fifteen days. The record was set in 2002 in just less than nine days. There are many dangers on the trip. The weather is very cold, and blinding snowstorms are common. The thin ice over rivers and lakes is often invisible. Wild moose get confused and sometimes trample dogs and sleds. Hungry wolves attack dogs and drivers. Both dogs and drivers can get sick. This is one of the most dangerous sporting events in the world.

Check Your Understanding

1. What is the best meaning of **musher**?
- a. a sled dog
- b. a race official
- c. a dog-team driver
- d. a lead dog

2. From the information in the passage, about how many dogs make up each sled team?
- a. 20
- b. 1,000
- c. 50
- d. 1

3. Which of the following is *not* a danger to race participants?
- a. a confused moose
- b. thin ice
- c. too much food
- d. wind storms and snowstorms

4. From the context of the passage, what is **diphtheria**?
- a. a trophy
- b. a disease
- c. a kind of dog
- d. dog food

/4

Warm-Up 27

Name ______________________________

The World Series

The World Series is the oldest yearly major sporting event in the United States. From 1903, when the series began, it has been played every fall except 1994. A labor strike canceled it that year. The reputation of the series was badly hurt in 1919. Eight members of the White Sox were accused of making a deal with gamblers to throw the series to the Reds. When the story came out, baseball's commissioner suspended the eight players for life.

The World Series has been marked with some special events. The Brooklyn Dodgers and the New York Yankees faced off in seven series in New York. Except for the series in 1955, the Yankees won the other six. The first time a World Series was won by a walk-off home run was in 1960. Pittsburgh Pirate Bill Mazeroski's homer broke a 9–9 tie in the 9th inning of the 7th game against the Yankees.

In 1956, Yankee Don Larsen pitched the only perfect game in World Series history. No Dodger reached first base. In 1977, Reggie Jackson hit three home runs on three **consecutive** turns at bat. He did it in the 6th game of a series against the Los Angeles Dodgers. In earlier years, Babe Ruth hit three home runs during a game in two different series. Babe also pitched for the Boston Red Sox to win two World Series titles in 1916 and 1918. Then he was sold to the Yankees and became a slugging outfielder. It would be the 21st century before the Red Sox would win another World Series.

Check Your Understanding

1. From the context of the passage, what is the best meaning of **consecutive**?
   a. all at once
   b. one at a time
   c. monstrous
   d. one after the other

2. Which of the following years is in the 21st century?
   a. 1916
   b. 2011
   c. 1918
   d. 1977

3. From the context of the passage, which of the following is a meaning for "suspended"?
   a. allowed to play
   b. hung
   c. not allowed to play
   d. all of the above

4. Which sentence from the passage is a topic sentence?
   a. second paragraph, first sentence
   b. second paragraph, last sentence
   c. third paragraph, first sentence
   d. third paragraph, last sentence

/4

Warm-Up

Name ____________________

28 The Golden Gate Bridge

The Golden Gate Bridge rises above San Francisco Bay. It is one of the great engineering achievements of the 20th century. The Golden Gate is one of the longest and most beautiful bridges in the world. It is a **suspension** bridge over 1.7 miles long. The bridge spans the Golden Gate Strait at the entrance to San Francisco Bay. It connects Marin County to San Francisco in Northern California. A tower stands at each end of the bridge. The distance between the two towers is 4,200 feet. The total length of the bridge is 8,981 feet. Each of the towers is about 1,120 feet from one end of the bridge. The bridge contains 88,000 tons of steel. There are 160,000 miles of wire in the two cables. The bridge is made of 390,000 cubic yards of concrete. One cubic yard is three feet long, three feet wide, and three feet high. The floor of the bridge is about 200 feet above water and 90 feet wide. This allows for six lanes and sidewalks. The chief engineer of the project was Joseph B. Strauss. The towers were designed by an architect named Irving Morrow. He also chose the unique rust-colored paint for the bridge. Golden Gate Bridge is designed to withstand very heavy tides. It also resists earthquakes and high winds. The idea for the bridge was first promoted in 1916 by a California journalist. California citizens, especially in the Bay area, soon recognized the value of a bridge like this. It would provide for better communication within the state. Business opportunities would be better. Construction began in 1933 during the Great Depression. It was completed four years later. The total cost was about thirty-five million dollars. Building the bridge provided thousands of jobs.

Check Your Understanding

1. From the context of the passage, what is the meaning of **suspension**?
   a. hanging in the air above water or land
   b. a mixture of water and a flavor
   c. flat on the ground or water
   d. sent home from school

2. How many times could the cable used in the bridge go back and forth from San Francisco to New York (3,000 miles each way)?
   a. 2 or 3 times
   b. more than 50 times
   c. more than 100 times
   d. 160,000 times

3. From the context of the passage, which word means "special, different, or unusual"?
   a. commerce
   b. suspension
   c. unique
   d. peninsula

4. Which of the following is an opinion and *not* a fact?
   a. It is a suspension bridge over 1.7 miles long.
   b. The Golden Gate is one of the longest and most beautiful bridges in the world.
   c. There are 160,000 miles of wire in the two cables.
   d. The Golden Gate Bridge rises above San Francisco Bay.

/4

Warm-Up 29

Name ____________________

Daytona International Speedway

The most famous track in automobile racing is the Daytona International Speedway. It is located in Daytona Beach, Florida. This track is as important to its sport as the Rose Bowl is to football or Yankee Stadium is to baseball. The Daytona Beach area has been called "the birthplace of speed." It got that name because car racers were running their cars on the twenty miles of hard-packed sand at this beach. This began in 1902. Stock car racing was born on these beaches. Auto races in the area became very popular in the years after World War II. In 1959, a new 2.5-mile-long modern course was completed. In addition, it had a new twist. This speedway was shaped like a curved triangle. It allowed fans in the grandstands to see approaching cars better. The raceway was banked a rather steep 31 degrees. This also improved viewing for the fans, and it increased the speed of the racing cars.

All other major sports end their seasons with a championship series. Auto racing is different. The racecar season starts in February with its most important racing event, the Daytona 500, a 500-mile-long race. Almost 200,000 fans attend this race. The grandstand at the racetrack has seats for 168,000 fans. Thousands of other fans in motor homes camp in the infield. The track speed record was set in February of 1980 at 177.6 miles per hour. One of the most famous racecar drivers is Richard Petty. He won the Daytona 500 a record ten times. However, driver Dale Earnhardt, Sr., lost nineteen years in a row. He finally won in 1998. In 2001, he was killed in the last lap of the race.

Check Your Understanding

1. Which part of the passage is described like a curved triangle?
   a. cars
   b. Daytona Speedway
   c. Daytona Beach
   d. infield

2. How many miles long is the Daytona 500?
   a. 2.5
   b. 500
   c. 200
   d. no limit

3. Which physical feature first attracted stock car racers to Daytona Beach?
   a. hurricanes
   b. wide roads
   c. the ocean
   d. dry, hard-packed sand on the beaches

4. Which of the following would be a good title for the passage?
   a. "The Birthplace of Automobile Racing"
   b. "Racing on Sand"
   c. "Watching a Race"
   d. "Dale Earnhardt Races"

/4

Warm-Up 30

Name ____________________

Hoover Dam

Hoover Dam was built between 1931 and 1936. It was one of the great successes of American engineering. The dam was built on the Colorado River at the border between Arizona and Nevada. Hoover Dam is 660 feet wide at the base and 726 feet high. Towers on the dam extend forty feet above the dam. Hoover Dam created Lake Mead. It is a **man-made** lake 115 miles long and about 589 feet deep. Lake Mead covers 247 square miles. The dam is important for preventing floods. The lake supplies water to homes, farms, and industries. The falling water from the dam can produce more than one billion watts of electric power. The dam supplies water to more than one million acres of farmland.

The dam was built during the Great Depression when many people could not find jobs. Hoover Dam cost forty-nine million dollars to build and provided jobs for thousands of workers. Building accidents on the dam took ninety-six lives. Many other employees were also seriously injured. Before the dam could be started, Boulder City had to be built to house the workers. Miles of highways and railroads had to be laid from the dam site to Boulder City and Las Vegas. The dam itself used more stone and similar materials than a pyramid. The dam was named for Herbert Hoover. He had suggested the idea in 1921. He also helped get the project approved by Congress in 1928. He was president when construction started.

Check Your Understanding

1. From the context of the passage, which word refers to a measurement of electrical power?
a. injured
b. acres
c. watts
d. project

2. What can you infer about the building of Hoover Dam?
a. Construction cost more in the 1930s than today.
b. Construction cost less in the 1930s than today.
c. The cost was about the same in the 1930s as today.
d. There is nothing that you can infer.

3. Which fact would support the information in the first paragraph?
a. Lake Mead supplies water for crops and people.
b. The dam helps farmers control floods.
c. There are seventeen power-producing turbines at the dam.
d. all of the above

4. From the context of the passage, what is an antonym for **man-made**?
a. artificial
b. natural
c. fake
d. free

/4

Scientifically Speaking

Warm-Up 1

Name ____________________

Vermin of the Skies

Some space scientists have called asteroids "vermin of the skies." They got this nickname because of their small size and the danger they can cause. "Vermin" is a term usually used for unpopular pests, such as rats, roaches, and lice. Asteroids are a large group of miniature planets. They orbit the sun between Mars and Jupiter. They are where most meteorites come from. These small space rocks travel through the solar system and sometimes hit Earth. On occasion, they cause great destruction.

Scientists first believed that asteroids were the remains of a planet. They thought that it had been destroyed when it hit another planet. Now asteroids are believed to be the pieces of a planet that never actually formed between Mars and Jupiter. It didn't become a planet because of the enormous pull of Jupiter's gravity.

Ceres, the largest asteroid, was first seen in 1801. It is about 580 miles in diameter. Pallas, the second largest asteroid, was discovered the following year. About 1,000 asteroids are twenty miles wide or greater. Astronomers estimate that as many as one million asteroids are between half a mile and twenty miles wide. Asteroids got their name because they look like points of light when seen through a telescope. Have you ever seen an asteroid?

Check Your Understanding

1. How big is the largest asteroid ever seen?
- a. 580 miles in diameter
- b. 850 miles in diameter
- c. half a mile wide
- d. twenty miles wide

2. Why are asteroids called "vermin of the skies"?
- a. They are known to have mice and rats living on them.
- b. They sometimes have a smaller size and cause damage.
- c. They look like mice through a telescope.
- d. People don't like asteroids.

3. What is the main idea of the passage?
- a. Astronauts should visit asteroids.
- b. Asteroids look like points of light in a telescope.
- c. Jupiter has a lot of gravitational force.
- d. Asteroids are small mini-planets that can produce meteorites.

4. Which piece of information about asteroids is least relevant to understanding asteroids?
- a. There are more than one million asteroids.
- b. Asteroids look like points of light in a telescope.
- c. Asteroids have been featured in some space movies.
- d. Parts of asteroids break off and become meteorites.

/4

Warm-Up 2

Name ______________________________

The Lost Planet

Many Americans were upset when astronomers removed Pluto from the list of planets. It is no longer the ninth planet in the solar system. They labeled it a dwarf planet along with a larger object named Eris. Both objects are located in a zone beyond Neptune called the Kuiper Belt. Dwarf planets are much smaller than the other eight planets.

Pluto was the only planet discovered by an American. An astronomer from Kansas named Clyde Tombaugh found it. He had carefully compared photos of an area of space beyond Neptune. This area was thought to contain a ninth planet. He spent more than 7,000 hours over more than two years comparing photographs of light. He was trying to discover the movement of a planet against the background stars. On February 18, 1930, Tombaugh discovered this movement. An eleven-year-old English schoolgirl won a contest to name the planet. She suggested Pluto, who is the god of the underworld in ancient myths.

Why was Pluto removed from the list of major planets? In a word—size. Charon, a moon orbiting Pluto, was discovered. It was about half the size of Pluto. Moons are not that large compared to the planets they orbit. Scientists were also able to determine Pluto's actual size, which was quite a bit smaller than originally thought. Pluto was found to be smaller than several moons, including our own. Its orbit was also very different from the other planets. Pluto is, of course, still there. It just doesn't have as big of a reputation anymore.

Check Your Understanding

1. What is the main idea of the passage?
- a. Pluto got smaller.
- b. Pluto is not a planet.
- c. There are reasons Pluto is no longer considered a planet.
- d. Pluto was discovered by an American.

2. Which of the following statements is an opinion and *not* a fact?
- a. Pluto was found to be smaller than several moons.
- b. Pluto was the only planet discovered by an American.
- c. Pluto should be considered a planet.
- d. A schoolgirl won the competition to name the planet.

3. What inference can you make about the description of a dwarf planet?
- a. Planets have to be bigger than most or all moons to be considered a conventional planet.
- b. Planets should be much larger than their own moon to be considered a regular planet.
- c. Planets should have conventional orbits, rather than eccentric ones, to be labeled a regular planet.
- d. all of the above

4. How did Pluto get its name?
- a. It was named for a child's pet.
- b. It was named for a cartoon dog.
- c. It was named for a god of the underworld.
- d. all of the above

/4

Warm-Up 3

Name ____________________

Rain

Rain is created in clouds when water vapor has evaporated from oceans, lakes, or wetlands. The clouds are filled with trillions of tiny specks of water vapor. These specks become attached to very small specks of dust, smoke, sand, pollen, salt, and other small bits in the air. A single rain droplet is formed by millions of these small water droplets hitting together.

The proper name for rain is *precipitation*, which includes snow, sleet, and hail, as well as rain. Most rain starts out as snow that melts before it hits the ground. Snow is ice crystals that form in clouds where the temperature is below zero. Sleet is a mixture of rain and melted snow. Rain starts when water drops inside clouds grow too large for air to support them. Cloud drops grow when wet air is swept higher into the air. There, it cools and gets heavier, causing it to fall. Raindrops can also grow by colliding with each other in tropical clouds or by growing on ice crystals in cooler air.

The world's rainiest place is a mountain in Hawaii that receives rain 350 days a year. The wettest land area is located in an area of Colombia in South America. It gets an average of over 463 inches a year. The longest known period without rain was from October 1903 to January 1918 in Arica, Chile.

Check Your Understanding

1. Which of the following is *not* an example of precipitation?
   a. rain
   b. snow
   c. wind
   d. sleet

2. Which of the following is an opinion and *not* a fact?
   a. The world's rainiest place is a mountain in Hawaii.
   b. Rain is created in clouds when water vapor has evaporated.
   c. Rain should make people feel good.
   d. Raindrops can grow by colliding with each other.

3. Which of the following will cause water droplets to condense and fall as rain?
   a. the sun
   b. clouds sweeping into cooler air
   c. lightning
   d. airplanes

4. What is the main idea of the second paragraph?
   a. Rain forms in clouds and falls when water condenses and becomes heavier than the surrounding air.
   b. There are places with a high average rainfall.
   c. Some places have little rain.
   d. Rain can fall in large amounts.

/4

Warm-Up 4

Name ____________________

Decibel Levels

The loudness of sounds in the environment is measured in units called decibels, or dB. At 0 dB, sound is not loud enough to be heard by humans. A falling leaf or feather would be rated at 0 dB. At 10 dB, the sound is so soft that you can barely hear it. A true whisper from a friend in the next seat would be a 10 on the scale. A louder whisper across a classroom would register at 30 or 40 dB. A normal conversation would be expressed at about 60 dB. A noisy classroom or cafeteria is in the 70 dB range. A jackhammer registers at about 80 dB. Every 10-degree increase in decibels is ten times as loud as the one before, so that 70 dB is 10 times as loud as 60 dB.

Noise above 70 dB is harmful to hearing and dangerous to the ears. Noise above 140 dB causes physical pain to your body. It may cause long-term injury to your ears if you often listen to this level of noise. Firecrackers can be as loud as 100 dB, and loud rock concerts and power saws are 110 dB or higher. A jet takeoff reaches 120 dB on the scale, as does a car horn at close range. An air-raid siren hits 140 dB, and a rocket takes off at 150 dB. At 145 dB, human eyeballs vibrate back and forth, and vision blurs. At 152 dB, the body feels severe pain in the joints. Throat vibrations caused by the sound can make swallowing difficult. Vibrations at 154 dB will pop a balloon, and 200 dB may result in death.

Check Your Understanding

1. According to the passage, what is the highest safe decibel level for humans?
   a. 130 dB
   b. 70 dB
   c. 110 dB
   d. 200 dB

2. At what decibel level does noise become physically painful and create a danger of long-term injury?
   a. 10 dB
   b. 140 dB
   c. 110 dB
   d. 70 dB

3. Which of the following is the most dangerous exposure for humans?
   a. firecrackers
   b. jet plane takeoff
   c. air-raid siren
   d. rocket takeoff

4. How much more powerful is a decibel level of 140 dB than a level of 130 dB?
   a. 2 times
   b. 10 times
   c. 100 times
   d. There is no way to tell.

/4

Warm-Up 5

Name ______________________________

Natural Chimneys

Black smokers are natural chimneys on the bottom of the ocean floor. They form on the seabed along ridges in the middle of an ocean where tectonic plates are moving apart. These are the giant plates that cause continents to drift slowly apart. They can also cause earthquakes or volcanoes.

Black smokers are hot water tubes affected by liquid rocks below the ocean. Seawater seeps through cracks along the ocean floor. This water is heated by the intensely hot liquid rock. This super-heated water dissolves minerals from the rocks. When the water is heated to these very high temperatures, the water is shot through tall stone tubes into the cold sea. Mineral deposits are left in these tubes. Some of them rise over 150 feet high on the ocean floor.

A large variety of creatures live in these totally dark ocean smokers. Tubeworms more than five feet long live there. They have no mouth or gut! They have more than 200,000 feathery tentacles and live on bacteria. Other creatures include shellfish and giant clams. Seawater travels through these black smokers just as it does throughout the oceans. Every drop of ocean water flows through a black smoker about every ten million years.

Check Your Understanding

1. From the context of the passage, what is a **black smoker**?
   a. a hot water tube on the ocean floor
   b. a fiery smoking hole in the ocean
   c. a tectonic plate
   d. a kind of sea creature
2. How often does all ocean water circulate through a black smoker?
   a. every year
   b. every million years
   c. every ten million years
   d. never
3. What is heating the water near black smokers?
   a. an earthquake
   b. liquid rock
   c. the sun
   d. tubeworms
4. Why would it be hard for scientists to personally touch and examine the tubeworms and black smokers?
   a. The hot water would be dangerous.
   b. The tubeworms might try to eat them.
   c. The pressure of the oceans at this depth would injure the scientists.
   d. both a and c

/4

Warm-Up 6

Name ____________________

Threats to Earth

Life as we know it exists on Earth because of special circumstances. Water and air are two important substances that support life. Temperatures are moderate over much of the planet. A huge variety of life exists in the form of both plants and animals. However, there are several things that could destroy life on Earth as we know it.

An unknown volcano, as much as one hundred times greater than any known in history, could erupt anywhere at any time with little or no warning. Large amounts of ash, dirt, deadly smoke, and lava would be pumped into the air. Sunlight would be shut out for many years by the clouds. Millions of plant and animal species would die. A volcano like this blew up thousands of years ago. It left only a few thousand humans alive.

A meteor is an asteroid that hits Earth. About six tons of meteorites fall into Earth's **atmosphere** every year. Most of them are burned up by the friction that is created when the speeding meteor blasts into the atmosphere. A few survive and hit Earth. They often create craters. About every 10,000 years, a large and highly damaging asteroid hits Earth. About every fifty to one hundred million years, an asteroid about six miles wide hits Earth. The dinosaurs were likely destroyed this way about sixty-five million years ago.

Check Your Understanding

1. From the context of the passage, what is the best meaning of **atmosphere**?

a. land and water
b. air and gases above a planet
c. meteor landing
d. dust and ash

2. Which information would be relevant to the passage?

a. Comet collisions can cause enormous damage.
b. There is a super-volcano under Yellowstone National Park.
c. A gamma ray burst in space could boil away Earth's atmosphere.
d. all of the above

3. Use the context of the passage to determine which fact stated below is *not* accurate.

a. Not all asteroids become meteors.
b. Some meteors do no damage to Earth.
c. Super-volcanoes happen about every ten years on Earth.
d. Blocking out the sun causes enormous damage to life on Earth.

4. Which of the following is essential to human life?

a. water
b. air
c. sunlight
d. all of the above

/4

Warm-Up 7

Name ______________________________

The First Professional Woman Astronomer

The first woman astronomer helped discover the planet Uranus. Caroline Herschel and her brother William were, at first, musicians. They were born in Germany. However, they lived and worked in England for most of their lives. William became **fascinated** by the telescope. At that time, it was a new invention. Because they were poor, William decided to build his own telescope. He even had to use horse manure as the mold for the telescope mirrors. He built his own four-foot wide, forty-foot long telescope. It was the largest telescope in the world at the time. Caroline helped her brother by spoon-feeding him while he ground the lenses for his telescopes.

In 1781, William discovered a new planet—Uranus. He did this using a telescope he built. It was the first planet discovered with a telescope. It was the first planet that had not been known to people in ancient times. It was much farther away than Saturn. So the discovery of Uranus doubled the known size of the solar system. During her lifetime, Caroline herself used the telescope. She discovered eight comets. Both Caroline and her brother were awarded honors. They were also given yearly pensions by King George III for their findings. Because of these awards, Caroline became the first professional female astronomer.

Check Your Understanding

1. Which of the following ideas can you infer from the passage?
   a. William and Caroline were trained at a university to study astronomy.
   b. Caroline and William were close friends who worked well together.
   c. Music and astronomy are similar subjects.
   d. William and Caroline were rich members of the nobility.

2. Which event made Caroline a professional astronomer instead of just an amateur student of the skies?
   a. helping William build a telescope
   b. getting a pension from King George III
   c. using a telescope
   d. discovering Uranus

3. Which detail in the passage strongly suggests that Caroline and her brother were very close friends and collaborators?
   a. William discovered Uranus.
   b. William made the largest telescope of its time.
   c. The king gave them both a pension.
   d. Caroline spoon-fed William while he ground the lens for a telescope.

4. From the context of the passage, what is the meaning of **fascinated**?
   a. lazy
   b. very interested in
   c. happy
   d. both a and b

/4

Warm-Up 8

Name ______________________________

Dangerous African Mammals

The male hippopotamus can weigh up to 7,000 pounds, the weight of three or more automobiles, and can run as fast as eighteen miles per hour. Hippos have enormous teeth, including tough, sharp tusks. Hippos can bite a man in half. They have quick tempers and will often target humans. They will even tip over boats and attack the passengers. Hippos kill a large number of humans in Africa every year.

The African buffalo is very dangerous. The oldest and strongest males can weigh 2,000 pounds and run as fast as thirty-five miles an hour. They have long, sharp horns and will gather in herds of more than 2,000 animals. They are extremely **aggressive** and can outrun lions, if they get a head start. The African buffalo will stalk and kill a human, whether the animal has been provoked or not. They will ambush a hunter by exploding out of a hidden area. Then they charge directly at the hunter. These buffalo will also mob lions, as well as their cubs.

Elephants are also very dangerous to humans. A male African elephant can weigh 11,000 pounds. That is the weight of more than five cars. Elephants will also kill other large animals, such as lions and rhinoceros. They charge their enemies and use their long tusks as weapons. African elephants kill as many as five hundred people a year. Choosing the most dangerous African animal would be hard, but you wouldn't want to be in the way of any of these large, powerful mammals.

Check Your Understanding

1. Which of the following has a similar meaning to **aggressive**?
   a. willing to run away
   b. ready to attack
   c. outrun
   d. both a and b

2. Which animal will attack and kill lions?
   a. African elephant
   b. African buffalo
   c. hippopotamus
   d. both a and b

3. Which piece of information provides support for the idea that buffalo are the most dangerous animals in Africa?
   a. They attack big game hunters with ease.
   b. They are good swimmers and their large ears allow them to hear well.
   c. They like to soak in water and can bite humans in half.
   d. They attack boats.

4. Which of these statements is an opinion and *not* a fact?
   a. Hippos attack people and boats.
   b. African buffalo are the most intelligent animals.
   c. Hippos are prettier than elephants.
   d. both b and c

/4

Warm-Up 9

Name ____________________

You Wouldn't Want to Live on Venus

Venus has the highest average temperature of any planet in the solar system. It reaches temperatures of 878°F. This is about eight to ten times as hot as Earth. Temperatures this high would melt lead and most other metals, not to mention people. The surface pressure of Venus is ninety times greater than Earth's. No human could stand the pressure without being smashed flat. It would equal the pressure felt by a human standing under half a mile of ocean water on our planet. The atmosphere is about 96 percent carbon dioxide. There is no breathable air. Any human would be burned to ashes and crushed to fragments immediately. An early Russian space probe landed on Venus. It was destroyed by the pressure and heat within thirty minutes.

Venus is the second planet in the solar system. Its average distance from the sun is about 67,000,000 miles. It is about a third closer than Earth's 93,000,000 miles. Venus is hotter than Mercury, the closest planet to the sun. Venus's carbon dioxide atmosphere traps heat and doesn't allow it to escape. It acts like a greenhouse, which traps heat and doesn't cool off. Because of this atmosphere, Venus is the brightest object in our sky, besides the moon and the sun. You might also get bored on Venus. A Venus day is equal to 243 Earth days. A Venus year is equal to 225 Earth days. Out of all the planets in the solar system, this is one planet you wouldn't want to visit.

Check Your Understanding

1. What is the most common gas in the atmosphere of Venus?
- a. oxygen
- b. nitrogen
- c. carbon dioxide
- d. argon

2. Which are the three brightest objects in our night sky?
- a. the sun, the moon, Mars
- b. Mercury, Venus, the sun
- c. Venus, the moon, Mars
- d. the moon, the sun, Venus

3. Why does the heat remain on Venus?
- a. It is held in by the carbon dioxide in the atmosphere.
- b. Gravity keeps the heat from escaping.
- c. It is very close to the sun.
- d. There are a lot of forest fires on Venus.

4. What would happen to astronauts landing on Venus?
- a. They would be crushed to bits by the pressure.
- b. They would be incinerated by the heat.
- c. They would be unable to breathe.
- d. all of the above

/4

Warm-Up 10

Name ____________________

The Heaviest Flying Bird

Some heavy birds, like the ostrich and emu, have lost the ability to fly. The heaviest flying bird is the great bustard. The male of this species can weigh up to forty-six pounds, about the same as a bulldog, while the lighter female can weigh up to eleven pounds. Great bustards live in much of Asia, Eastern Europe and parts of Northern Africa. Some people in these areas even raise bustards on farms. Great bustards eat a lot of plants and especially prefer vegetables, such as kale and cabbages. They will also eat many kinds of insects, as well as spiders, frogs, and small rodents, such as voles.

Great bustards are able to fly because they have strong wings that they must flap all the time. Unlike lighter birds, they do not glide through the air and, in fact, would fall like stones if they tried. The male bustard has a wingspan of up to seven feet. Bustards are good runners, too. The main predator of great bustards is the fox, but the bustard can escape it by flying or running because it is faster than a fox. Great bustards are usually silent, but they can bark at other males during fights.

The female lays two or three eggs that hatch in a few weeks. A chick weighs about as much as a lemon or an orange when born and can fly by the time it is three months old. It stays with the mother for about a year and lives for approximately ten to fifteen years.

Check Your Understanding

1. From the context of the passage, what can you infer about the development of young bustards?
   a. Chicks need the protection of older bustards.
   b. Bustards aren't safe from predators in the first year after birth.
   c. Bustard chicks need to fly for protection against predators.
   d. all of the above

2. About how much heavier is the male bustard than the female?
   a. about twenty pounds
   b. about three pounds
   c. about four times as heavy
   d. about one hundred pounds

3. Which of these geographic areas is *not* a native home to great bustards?
   a. Eastern Europe
   b. Northern Africa
   c. North America
   d. Asia

4. From the context of the passage, how can you tell that the adult bustards are good parents?
   a. They feed their young.
   b. The young stay with their parents for a year.
   c. The bustards are capable fliers.
   d. The bustards are usually silent.

/4

Warm-Up 11

Name ______________________________

Bioluminescence at Sea

In nature, light can come from the sun, the stars, lightning, and wildfires. Even the reflection from the moon provides light. However, another source of light can be produced in the oceans from living animals that create their own light. This process is called **bioluminescence**, or "light from life." Animals that make their own light are called bioluminescent. Fireflies are an example of insects living on land that make their own light, but most of these creatures live in the oceans.

There are pencil-point-sized creatures that glow when they are disturbed by anything in the sea, from a boat to a bubble. Some shellfish the size of birdseed flash blue lights to attract mates. The light organ of a flashlight fish is about the size of a bean. However, it carries about a billion bacteria. They provide light for it to hunt for food. Many deep-sea fish have lights on their bellies, sides, or tails. Some jellyfish glitter with their own light, which they use to attract prey or blind an enemy.

Squid are masters of deception with light. They are able to create many special light effects with bacteria living on their skin and special cells of different colors. They can make false eyespots, zebra stripes, silver flanks, and glowing eyebrows. They can even squirt light-producing chemicals into the water to hide a quick getaway from their enemies.

Check Your Understanding

1. From the context of the passage, what is the best meaning of **bioluminescence**?
   a. reflected light
   b. light from the stars
   c. light created by living organisms
   d. starlight
2. Which of these defensive light effects is used by squid?
   a. false eyespots
   b. zebra stripes
   c. squirting light-producing chemicals into the water
   d. all of the above
3. Using the context of the passage, which land-based insect is bioluminescent?
   a. housefly
   b. cricket
   c. squid
   d. firefly
4. Which of the following do *not* help create bioluminescent effects in ocean creatures?
   a. bacteria
   b. special cells
   c. clouds
   d. all of the above

/4

Warm-Up 12

Name ____________________

Lightning

A lightning bolt is a huge electric spark created in a thundercloud. The spark leaps across the sky. Water droplets and ice crystals crash together in a thundercloud. They create static electricity. There are two electrical charges in the cloud. Lighter positive charges whirl around at the top of a cloud, and heavier negative charges are at the bottom of the cloud. Lightning is created when a positive charge from the ground and a negative charge at the bottom of the cloud jump together. Then electrical energy is released. A flash of lightning can contain one billion volts of electricity. Lightning heats the area around it even hotter than the sun. Forked, zigzag, and sheet lightning are the most common shapes.

About 1,000 people a year are injured by lightning, and about one hundred people a year are killed. People die from burns, shock, or heart attacks. To protect yourself from lightning during thunderstorms, try to get inside a building. If you can't find protection, stay away from trees, especially from a single tree. A tree or pole is the highest point. It will attract lightning because it provides the shortest path to the ground. Do not hold umbrellas or other metal objects because they attract the electric charge. Lightning does strike the same place twice and often many times. For example, tall structures like skyscrapers and towers are struck many times a year. As long as you know what to do when there's lightning in the sky, you will be safe.

Check Your Understanding

1. What two charges of electric energy are necessary to create lightning?
- a. two positive charges
- b. a neutral charge and a positive charge
- c. two negative charges
- d. a negative charge and a positive charge

2. From the context of the passage, which of the following should you stand next to during a thunderstorm?
- a. a huge tree
- b. a flagpole
- c. a tractor in an empty field
- d. none of the above

3. Which of the following is a good example of a topic sentence?
- a. paragraph one, last sentence
- b. paragraph one, first sentence
- c. paragraph two, first sentence
- d. both b and c

4. Is this sentence correct?
Lightning is created when a positive charge on the ground is attracted to a negative charge at the bottom of a thundercloud.
- a. yes
- b. no
- c. sometimes
- d. never

/4

Warm-Up 13

Name ______________________________

The Largest Volcano on Earth

The largest volcano in the world is located in the western United States. The last explosion occurred 600,000 years ago. It blew away about sixty miles of mountains. It buried nineteen western states under several feet of ash. It also covered parts of Canada and Mexico with ash. The blast wiped out almost every living thing in a wide area. That explosion was 1,000 times greater than when Mount St. Helens blew.

This giant volcano is sitting under Yellowstone National Park. It is just about the size of the two-million-acre park. The first known blowup happened over sixteen million years ago. This volcano has blown up about a hundred times since. The blasts occur about 600,000 years apart. No known volcano in history compares to the explosions that have occurred in Yellowstone. The damage caused by yet another explosion would be hard to imagine.

A thin rock surface in Yellowstone covers a huge lake of hot liquid rock beneath the surface. This boiling hot pool of liquid rock is about forty-five miles across and eight miles deep. It has lifted Earth's crust about one-third of a mile higher than it would normally be. This heat creates the hot springs, geysers, and mud pots in this popular national park.

Check Your Understanding

1. Where is the lake of hot liquid rock?
   a. sixty miles beneath the surface
   b. in Canada
   c. beneath the rock crust in Yellowstone
   d. above the rock crust in Yellowstone

2. Where is the largest volcano in history located?
   a. Mount St. Helens
   b. Yellowstone National Park
   c. Canada
   d. both a and b

3. Which of these features is present at Yellowstone for people to observe?
   a. geysers
   b. mud pots
   c. exploding volcanoes
   d. both a and b

4. What is the purpose of the passage?
   a. to inform readers
   b. to ask questions
   c. to entertain readers
   d. to stop a volcano

/4

Warm-Up 14

Name ______________________________

Jupiter—The Planetary Giant

Jupiter is the fifth planet in the solar system in distance from the sun. It is by far the largest object in the solar system, other than the sun. Jupiter contains more than twice the mass of all the other planets combined. If Jupiter were hollow, more than 1,000 Earths could fit inside this gas giant. Jupiter's mass is about 318 times the mass of Earth. Jupiter is sometimes considered to be a "failed sun." However, it is at least eighty times too small to ignite as a star.

There are four main gases in Jupiter's atmosphere. Beneath layers of these gases, Jupiter has oceans of liquid nitrogen about 12,000 miles deep. Beneath the oceans, there is probably a solid core of rock and iron about the size of Earth. Jupiter spins on its axis so fast that its day is only about ten hours long. However, the rapid spinning makes belts of winds circle the planet. These belts created a giant storm called the Great Red Spot, which has been blowing over the planet for more than three hundred years. The average temperature on Jupiter is about 225°F colder than Earth.

Jupiter has sixty-three known moons and thousands of huge rocks orbiting the planet. The first four moons were discovered by Galileo. Two of them are a little smaller than Earth's moon in diameter. One of them is the largest moon in the solar system. It is larger than the planet Mercury. Jupiter's fourth moon is about the size of Mercury. The remaining moons are much smaller.

Check Your Understanding

1. According to the passage, what is probably at the center of Jupiter?
a. helium
b. rock
c. ammonia
d. methane

2. What produced the Great Red Spot?
a. oceans
b. belts of wind
c. rapid spinning of the planet
d. both b and c

3. According to the passage, how many moons orbit Jupiter?
a. sixty-three
b. ten
c. twenty-four
d. fifty-one

4. Why would Jupiter be impossible for humans to live on?
a. It has the largest moon in the solar system.
b. Its days are ten hours long.
c. The average temperature is too cold.
d. all of the above

/4

Name ______________________________

Warm-Up 15

Tide Pools

Tide pools are pockets of ocean water left on the coastal edges of the oceans when the tide goes out. They are sometimes small puddles in sand or mud with deeper pools between rocks. Tides are created by the gravitational pull of the moon and sun on ocean water. The ocean water reaches its highest point on the coast during high tide. Water fills most pools and covers most tide-pool life during high tide. During low tide, ocean water reaches its lowest point, and you can see many animals in the pools or stranded on the sand. The tides are particularly low during new moon and full moon periods.

There are three main types of algae living in tide pools: green, brown, and red. Sea lettuce is a kind of green and leafy algae. Irish moss is the name of one type of red algae. Rockweed is a type of common brown algae. Clams and snails are kinds of mollusks found in tide pools. Red, green, pink, and purple sea anemones, looking like flowers, often cling to rocks in the pools. Jellyfish shaped like small umbrellas float across the surface of water. They sting and eat small ocean animals. Crabs, barnacles, sea stars (starfish), sea urchins, and worms of many colors can be seen.

Do not remove any tide-pool creatures. Many of them are now endangered species because they have been gathered by people and taken from their native environment. Tide pools are natural laboratories for people of all ages to study nature.

Check Your Understanding

1. Which kind of tide-pool life is classified as a mollusk?
   a. a sea star
   b. a clam
   c. algae
   d. a sea urchin
2. When is the best time to see many forms of ocean life in tide pools?
   a. during high tide
   b. during low tide
   c. anytime
   d. at night
3. Which of the following is an opinion and *not* a fact?
   a. Tide pools are natural laboratories for people of all ages to study nature.
   b. There are three main types of algae living in tide pools.
   c. The ocean water reaches its highest point on the coast during high tide.
   d. Rockweed is a type of common brown algae.
4. What are sea anemones compared to in the passage?
   a. sea stars
   b. flowers
   c. umbrellas
   d. rocks

/4

Warm-Up **16** Name ____________________

The Extinct Quagga

The quagga went extinct in 1887 when the last surviving member of the species died in a zoo. An animal is extinct if all the members of the species are dead. The quagga was an animal similar to a horse. It was native to the plains of South Africa. It looked like a cross between a horse and a zebra. The front of the animal was striped like a zebra. The rear was brown like a horse.

In the 1980s, scientists studied strands of DNA from a piece of quagga skin found in a museum. (*DNA* is a chemical found in each living thing. It is different and special for each species.) They discovered that the quagga was so closely related to the zebra that both species were from the same family line. They could tell that both species probably developed from a common animal that lived before they existed. These scientists believed that all of the genes that were a part of the quagga's DNA exist in the living cells of wild zebras that still roam the African plains.

These scientists started a program to bring back the quagga by selecting zebras with fewer stripes on the rear of their bodies to mate. They hope to eventually discover one or more of these baby zebras whose DNA matches what they found in the quagga skin. If this experiment works, it will be the first species ever brought back to life.

Check Your Understanding

1. What is the name of the chemical compound that codes genetic information in genes?
 a. RNA
 b. quagga
 c. DNA
 d. all of the above

2. Which animal is the quagga most closely related to?
 a. horse
 b. zebra
 c. camel
 d. both b and c

3. What is the main idea of the passage?
 a. The quagga has been extinct for over one hundred years.
 b. The horse is related to the quagga.
 c. Scientists are trying to recreate the quagga by breeding closely related zebras.
 d. The zebra is related to the quagga.

4. Which of the following pieces of information is least relevant to the passage?
 a. Quaggas became extinct in recent times.
 b. The quagga is closely related to the zebra and the horse.
 c. A movie was made about bringing back extinct species.
 d. DNA is a chemical compound that codes genetic information.

/4

Warm-Up 17

Name ____________________

The KT Event

Scientists believe that a terrible disaster occurred about sixty-five million years ago. A meteor about six miles wide crashed into Mexico. It formed a crater more than one hundred miles wide. This giant meteor was traveling more than thirty miles per second when it hit Earth. The energy from this collision would have equaled at least one billion megatons of dynamite. (A *megaton* is one million tons.) It is called the KT event.

This KT collision created huge fragments of the meteor that were thrown back into the atmosphere. These giant pieces reentered like more meteors in other places on the planet. The temperature of Earth's atmosphere was superheated for several hours. Plants and animals that were out in the open were burned to ashes. This created thick clouds of black soot in the air. The air was choked for weeks with thick layers of smoke, dust, and other debris. This layer is seen in the fossil record.

Sunlight could not get through this layer for months. This caused a very long winter that lasted all over the world and harmed even more species. At least 70 percent of all living species, including the dinosaurs, were wiped out by this event. Some large crocodiles and other water-based creatures survived. The KT event eventually led to many new species. These included mammals, which developed rapidly.

Check Your Understanding

1. What would scientists examine in the fossil record?
   - a. rocks
   - b. fossils
   - c. books
   - d. both a and b
2. Why might water-based animals be more likely to survive the KT collision?
   - a. Deep water might have protected them from the fires.
   - b. Some sea creatures can tolerate wide ranges of temperature.
   - c. Some sea creatures get oxygen from the water.
   - d. all of the above
3. Which of these facts is relevant to the passage?
   - a. There have been several other giant extinctions on Earth.
   - b. Many snakes and crocodiles survived the KT event.
   - c. Every dinosaur was destroyed.
   - d. all of the above
4. What can you infer from reading the passage?
   - a. The KT event changed Earth forever.
   - b. We can avoid future collisions like the KT event.
   - c. Scientists are sure of all the results of the collision.
   - d. People would survive a KT event today.

/4

Warm-Up **18**

Name ______________________________

Animal Vision

Humans and most animals have eyes, which are organs that allow them to see their surroundings. Eyes have sensors that detect light. Insects and crabs have compound eyes. A compound eye is composed of hundreds of tiny individual lenses. Each lens sees an image, and the creature's brain creates one image by putting all of the individual images together.

Many animal eyes have a pupil, a slit in the middle of the eyes. This opening gets larger and smaller to let in different amounts of light. Nocturnal animals like owls have large eyes with pupils that can open very wide. This lets in as much light as possible. Human pupils let in less light than owls, for example. Plant-eating animals with eyes on the sides of their head have good side vision. It allows them to keep an eye out for predators while eating.

Cats, nocturnal animals, and some deep-sea fish have a shiny layer at the back of their eyes. This layer acts as a mirror and collects whatever light is available. When you see a cat's eyes shining in the night, it is simply light reflecting off this layer. Some predators and tree-dwelling animals have vision that allows them to focus on objects or prey in the distance. Hawks and falcons have excellent distance vision. Humans have more limited distance vision.

Monkeys, apes, and humans have other vision advantages. Each eye views things from a slightly different angle. The brain joins the two views to form a 3-D image.

Check Your Understanding

1. Which animals have a layer at the back of the eyes that acts like a mirror?
   a. deep-sea fish
   b. owls
   c. monkeys
   d. plant-eating animals

2. Which type of vision can be found in humans?
   a. 3-D vision
   b. excellent distance vision
   c. good side vision
   d. excellent night vision

3. Which creatures see best at night?
   a. animals with good side vision
   b. nocturnal animals
   c. animals with compound eyes
   d. monkeys

4. What is the main idea of the passage?
   a. There is only one kind of animal vision.
   b. Animals see the same way people see.
   c. Animals have many different types of vision.
   d. People see better than animals.

/4

Warm-Up

19

Name ____________________

Mercury

Mercury is the closest planet to the sun. It is much smaller than Earth and has only one-third the gravity of Earth. Therefore, a one hundred-pound person would only weigh thirty-eight pounds on Mercury. It has very little atmosphere because of its lower gravity. It is strongly affected by being so close to the sun. The daytime temperature of Mercury reaches 800°F above zero. At night, it drops to 350°F below zero. This is twice as cold as the coldest temperature ever known on Earth. Mercury does not really have seasons. Unlike Earth, Mercury has almost no tilt to its axis. In addition, the sun shines strongest on the equator of Mercury all year long.

Mercury looks a little like the moon because of the many craters formed when it was hit by **asteroids** billions of years ago. One crater was formed when a large asteroid smashed into it. It had such force that the impact formed mountains on the other side of the planet.

Mercury moves fast and makes four journeys around the sun in the course of one Earth year. (The Romans named the planet after the swift messenger of the gods called Mercury.) It moves so rapidly that it is only seen from Earth six times a year for two-week periods. It can be seen either just before or after sunset. When Mercury moves between Earth and the sun, it looks like a tiny black dot crossing the sun's path.

Check Your Understanding

1. What is the author's purpose in writing the passage?
- a. to convince a reader to go to Mercury
- b. to inform the reader about Mercury
- c. to offer advice on space travel
- d. to encourage space travel

2. From the context of the passage, what is an **asteroid**?
- a. a massive piece of rock moving through space
- b. a kind of spaceship
- c. a part of the sun
- d. a planet

3. What is the gravity on Earth of a person weighing one hundred pounds?
- a. 38 pounds
- b. 100 pounds
- c. 800 pounds
- d. 350 pounds

4. Which of the following pieces of information would be relevant to the passage?
- a. Mercury passes directly between the sun and Earth only thirteen times each century.
- b. A day on Mercury lasts 136 Earth days.
- c. If Earth were the size of a baseball, Mercury would be the size of a golf ball.
- d. all of the above

/4

Warm-Up

20

Name ____________________

Animal Messages

Animals have their own methods of communication. You'll notice them if you pay attention and learn the languages.

Many animals use color-coding to send messages. The bright orange colors on a ladybug, a cinnabar caterpillar, and the monarch butterfly tell some predators that the insect tastes bad. A toad may snap up one ladybug on its tongue and start to swallow it before it comes flying out. It won't strike at a second ladybug. Some butterflies and other insects show the colors of these awful-tasting insects. Peacocks, robins, frigate birds, and many other male birds will display their colorful chests as a way of attracting a female mate.

A female silkworm moth will release a scent when it is ready to mate. Many moths use this perfume signal. Male crickets and grasshoppers attract mates by rubbing the legs and wings together to make an attractive chirping sound. This is called *stridulation*.

Honeybees do a figure-eight "waggle dance" in the air to indicate where food may be found. Dominant wolves and dogs in a group have their ears up and teeth bared to indicate strength. Less powerful animals keep their ears flat and crouch or roll over on their backs. Skunks may send the most obvious message. A skunk will stamp its feet and raise its tail to warn enemies to leave it alone. Can you think of other kinds of messages that animals send?

Check Your Understanding

1. Which word refers to an insect rubbing its legs and wings together?
- a. frigate
- b. waggle
- c. stridulation
- d. display

2. What message does a "waggle dance" send?
- a. the location of the hive
- b. the location of food
- c. the location of a new queen
- d. the location of humans

3. How do toads, frogs, birds, and other creatures learn to *not* eat ladybugs and monarch butterflies?
- a. Their speed warns them.
- b. Their color warns them.
- c. Their taste warns them.
- d. both b and c

4. What can you infer from reading the passage?
- a. Ladybugs probably don't taste good to many predators.
- b. Many animals would rather warn their enemies than fight.
- c. Many animals can communicate without thinking.
- d. all of the above

/4

Warm-Up 21

Name ______________________________

The Human Brain

Your brain is the command center for almost all of your activities—thinking, moving, and breathing. It coordinates the different parts of your body. Your brain holds more information right now than a million full sets of encyclopedias. Most of the information relates to your life, your body, your experiences, and what you've learned.

Your brain looks like a large, gray, wrinkled walnut. It consists of over ten billion connected nerve cells. There are three main parts of the human brain. The largest and most important part is the cerebrum, which controls the senses, feelings, and thinking aspects of your life, as well as memory and speech. Most of the work you do in school involves this part of the brain. The cerebrum also controls the cerebellum, the part of the brain responsible for muscle use, coordination, and balance in the body. The brain stem controls functions such as breathing and heartbeat.

Your brain has two sides called **hemispheres**. They control different actions and the opposite sides of the body. In right-handed people, the left side of the brain controls speech, language, and logical thought. The right side specializes in recognizing objects, controlling emotions, and creative ideas. In left-handed people, these roles are reversed. Protect your brain. You need it for a lifetime!

Check Your Understanding

1. Which of the following is the best topic sentence in the passage?
   a. paragraph one, first sentence
   b. paragraph one, last sentence
   c. paragraph two, first sentence
   d. paragraph two, last sentence
2. From the context of the passage, what is a **hemisphere**?
   a. the top of the brain
   b. the bottom of the brain
   c. one side of the brain
   d. the cerebrum
3. If you are left-handed, which side of the brain controls your speech, language, and thought?
   a. the right side
   b. the left side
   c. the cerebrum
   d. the cerebellum
4. Which of the following is *not* a main part of the brain?
   a. cerebrum
   b. cerebellum
   c. brain stem
   d. skull

/4

Warm-Up 22

Name ____________________

Snow

Snow is composed of ice crystals. These crystals fall from clouds in cold weather when the air is too cold to melt the ice crystals into rain. In most of the world outside the very hot tropics, most rain starts to fall as snow but melts to rain on the way down. The heaviest snowfalls occur when the air temperature is close to the freezing point at 32°F.

For this reason, more snow falls on the northern United States than at the North Pole because it is too cold at the North Pole for snow to fall. Snow can be as much as 90 percent air. For this reason, snow helps to keep the ground warm and protect some plants from extreme cold. Because so much of the snow is composed of air, it takes about ten inches of snow to equal the amount of water in one inch of rain.

All snowflakes are six-sided crystals, with some occasional needles or columns. One farmer and amateur scientist photographed thousands of snowflakes through a microscope. He was trying to find two identical flakes. Neither he nor anyone else ever has. Snow often melts slowly because the white color reflects sunlight away. The most snow in a single storm in the United States was 189 inches. It occurred at Mount Shasta, California, in February 1959. Antarctica is buried in an average of two-and-a-half miles of snow.

Check Your Understanding

1. According to the passage, most rain starts to fall as snow but melts to rain on the way down in most of the world except
   a. the desert.
   b. the tropics.
   c. the city.
   d. Antarctica.
2. When does the heaviest snowfall usually occur?
   a. when the temperature is near 0°F
   b. when the temperature is as cold as the North Pole
   c. when the temperature is just about freezing
   d. when the temperature is above 50°F
3. About how much air is in snow?
   a. 90 percent
   b. 10 percent
   c. none
   d. 100 percent
4. Which of the following would be the best title for the passage?
   a. "How Snowflakes Are Formed"
   b. "Facts About Snow"
   c. "Ice and Snow"
   d. "The Heaviest Snowfall"

/4

Warm-Up 23

Name ______________________________

Tornadoes

A tornado is a whirling mass of air. It is a long tube of wind constantly turning around at very high speeds. It reaches down from the bottom of a storm cloud to the ground. The circling wind sucks up dust, loose material, and other things into a large funnel cloud. This cloud is shaped like a giant cone. It's less than two miles across and often as small as 240 feet across the center. Tornadoes are far smaller than hurricanes, but they can be very powerful. A terrible tornado in March of 1925 traveled 219 miles through the states of Missouri, Illinois, and Indiana. It blew at speeds as high as seventy-three miles per hour. This tornado killed 695 people and an unknown number of animals. The storm also destroyed 15,000 homes. It is considered the worst tornado in our history. The highest wind speed ever recorded on Earth was 318 miles per hour. This was inside the cone of a tornado in Oklahoma in May 1999. It killed four people and ruined 250 homes. Tornado season in the United States runs from February to May. Tornadoes are most common in the central and plains states, as well as the gulf states. Tornadoes are ranked by a system called the Fujita Scale. A mild F0 rating indicates little damage. A powerful F4 rating means severe damage. This damage includes houses destroyed, cars thrown around, and many objects hurled like missiles. The **rare** F5 rating occurs when buildings are lifted off their foundations and blown away and cars become weapons. F6 tornadoes are even more rare and destructive.

Check Your Understanding

1. From the context of the passage, which of the following is the least destructive tornado on the Fujita Scale?
   a. F6
   b. F4
   c. F1
   d. F5

2. Which of the following is a feature of a tornado?
   a. a rotating tube of wind
   b. a great deal of rain
   c. a narrow path of great destruction
   d. both a and c

3. From the context of the passage, which is the best antonym for **rare**?
   a. unknown
   b. awful
   c. evil
   d. common

4. From the context of the passage, which of the following creates the destructive force of a tornado?
   a. heavy rain
   b. the whirling wind in the center
   c. cold air
   d. flying cars

/4

Warm-Up 24

Name ____________________

The Laws of Motion

The three important laws of motion were first clearly stated by the great scientist Isaac Newton. The first law of motion states that an object at rest will remain at rest until it is acted on by a force. It also says that an object in motion will remain in motion at the same speed and in the same direction until a force acts on the object. In simple terms, a baseball sitting on a shelf will remain unmoved until someone places it in play. A baseball moving through the air will be acted on by the friction of the air and soon fall to the ground.

The second law of motion states that the speed of a moving object depends on how heavy the object being moved is and how hard it is being pushed or pulled by a force. The greater the force acting on an object, the more it will speed up. A powerful batter swinging a large, heavy bat will make a baseball move much faster than a small child with a plastic bat. The heavier an object is, the less the object will be moved by a force. Heavy rocks will not move as fast as a tennis ball when hit by the same force.

The third law of motion states that for every action there is an equal and opposite reaction. This means that a rocket moves forward by the action of the hot gases pushing out from it. The reaction happens when the rocket lifts off. A bouncing ball also shows this third law of motion. Try these out for yourself at recess or at home.

Check Your Understanding

1. The third law of motion states that for every action
   a. an object does something.
   b. there is an opposite reaction.
   c. there is an equal and opposite reaction.
   d. an object remains at rest.
2. A tennis ball bouncing off a garage floor best illustrates which law of motion?
   a. the first law of motion
   b. the second law of motion
   c. the third law of motion
   d. the fourth law of motion
3. A batter hitting a thrown ball best illustrates which law of motion?
   a. the first law of motion
   b. the second law of motion
   c. the third law of motion
   d. the first and second laws of motion
4. A golfer hitting a ball off a tee best illustrates which law of motion?
   a. the first law of motion
   b. the second law of motion
   c. the third law of motion
   d. the fourth law of motion

/4

Warm-Up 25

Name ______________________________

Clouds

Clouds are classified by their shapes and their heights above the ground. Although there are ten identified cloud types, there really are only three basic types of clouds: cumulus, stratus, and cirrus. *Cumulus* comes from the Latin word for "heap" or "pile." Cumulus clouds look like fluffy, whipped mashed potatoes. The size of the cloud depends on the amount of moisture in the air, as well as how quickly the air rises. Most cumulus clouds don't bring rain and lie below 6,000 feet. They are sparkling white at the top and sometimes have a light gray hue at the base.

Cirrus comes from a Latin word, which translates to a "lock of hair." Cirrus clouds are very high, often three to seven miles above the ground, and are wispy, thin, and look like there is little substance to them. They are formed by ice crystals, and sunlight can pass through these crystals with ease. *Stratus* gets its name from a Latin word meaning "spread out." Stratus clouds are flat, thick, and usually the lowest of the three types of clouds. Thick fog, for example, is a stratus cloud.

The rest of the cloud names are combinations of the three basic types. Nimbostratus clouds are dark, low-lying, and bring a lot of moisture as rain or snow. Cloud types such as altostratus and altocumulus are high in the sky. Cumulonimbus clouds look like an upside-down clothing iron high in the sky and can produce heavy precipitation, thunderstorms, tornadoes, and hail. What kinds of clouds are in the sky today?

Check Your Understanding

1. What kind of weather comes with clouds that have "nimbus" or "nimbo" in them?
   a. sunny
   b. wet and stormy
   c. dry
   d. foggy
2. Which clouds are formed of ice crystals high in the sky?
   a. cumulus
   b. stratus
   c. nimbostratus
   d. cirrus
3. Which clouds can bring tornadoes and thunderstorms?
   a. cumulonimbus
   b. cirrus
   c. cumulus
   d. altocumulus
4. Which of the following would be irrelevant to the passage?
   a. In 1888, twenty-six people were killed by a hailstorm in India.
   b. Clouds do not always bring storms.
   c. Altostratus clouds are thin and create a colored ring around the sun and the moon.
   d. Nimbostratus clouds often bring rain.

/4

Warm-Up **26** Name ____________________

Lions

Lions, like all cats, belong to a group of mammals called *felines*. They live in groups called *prides*. A pride may contain four to six adults and their cubs. Male lions usually weigh between 330 and 420 pounds. The job of male lions is to protect the pride from enemies. They also have to look after the young when the females are hunting. Male lions have manes of thick hair that protect them during fights and allow them to look larger and more dangerous to enemies, such as other male lions or hyenas. Adult males stay with a pride only a few years before they are defeated and sent away from the pride by stronger, younger males.

Lions hunt using their razor-sharp teeth, powerful claws, great agility, and sharp senses. Lions generally hunt only when they are hungry. Female lions do all of the hunting. However, the male insists on eating first from any kill. He will not allow any member of the pride to eat, even the female who did the hunting, until he has eaten his fill. A male lion may eat up to sixty-five pounds at one time, and then it may not need to eat for several days. Lions spend most of their time sleeping, often for twenty hours a day. Lions used to be widespread throughout Asia and India, but now only a few survive in a protected reserve in India. Lions **flourish** on the plains of Africa where they kill large prey, such as zebras.

Check Your Understanding

1. Which term refers to a place where wild animals are protected from human hunters?
a. flourish
b. reserve
c. felines
d. pride

2. Which sentence correctly describes one difference between male and female lions?
a. Males do the hunting while females care for the young.
b. Females fight for control of the pride while the males eat.
c. Females do the hunting, but the males eat first.
d. Males and females have razor-sharp teeth and powerful claws.

3. From the context of the passage, what is the meaning of **flourish**?
a. to wave back and forth
b. to eat well and survive
c. to die off
d. to run fast

4. What is the name for a group of lions living together?
a. mane
b. pride
c. felines
d. family

/4

Warm-Up 27

Name ______________________________

Water

Water is among the most important compounds on Earth. Plants, animals, and people could not live without many sources of water. The oceans of the world are giant engines that produce fresh water as rain and snow through the water cycle. Only 3% of the water on Earth is fresh water. The other 97% of the water is salt water in the oceans. Even most of the fresh water is locked up in glaciers and ice caps.

Water is the only substance that can be found as a solid (ice), liquid (water), and gas (steam or water vapor) within the normal range of Earth's temperatures. Water freezes at 32°F and boils at 212°F. Between those two temperatures, water flows as a liquid. The density of water is greatest at 39°F. This means that the most water can fit into a specific space at this temperature.

Ice is much less dense than liquid water. This is why ice forms on the surface of lakes and why icebergs and ice cubes float rather than sink. Water is unique in that it expands when it freezes. This causes water pipes to break during extremely cold winter weather. Water expands in an ice cube tray when it freezes, and the ice cube rises over the surface of the tray.

Check Your Understanding

1. What is the author's purpose in writing the passage?
   a. to encourage water usage
   b. to inform readers about the value and properties of water
   c. to compare water to air
   d. to entertain the reader

2. What does water do when it freezes?
   a. It expands.
   b. It gets more dense.
   c. It gets less dense.
   d. both a and c

3. Which of the following would be the best title for the passage?
   a. "Water Is Wet"
   b. "The Importance and Nature of Water"
   c. "Save Water"
   d. "Why Water Is Dense"

4. Which of the following offers true comparisons of liquid water and ice?
   a. Liquid water is denser than ice.
   b. Ice expands more than liquid water.
   c. Ice will not float.
   d. both a and b

/4

Warm-Up 28

Name ______________________________

The Human Eye

Light enters the eye through the cornea at your outer eye. The pupil either **dilates** or constricts, depending on the amount of available light. The lens keeps the image in focus. The retina at the back of your eyes contains about 125 million rods and 7 million cones. These are nerve cells that are sensitive to light. The retina is about as thick as a very thin sheet of paper. The eye has special cells sensitive to red, green, and blue light. Your brain can put different amounts of these colored lights together in order to see about ten million different shades of color. The lens of your eye is about the size of a small bean when you are a child, but it will grow larger as you age. Your lens is made up of layers of cells wrapped like an onion. The nerves in your eyes carry more information to your brain than most computers could handle.

If you look upwards and sideways toward a light-colored object, you may see tiny floating objects swimming in your eyes. These particles are very small substances that are actually inside your eyes. Your eye muscles move more than 100,000 times a day and are in constant motion, even when you are sleeping. You blink about 5,000 times a day. You spend a half-hour just blinking. With every blink, you bathe your eyes with a fluid that protects them from damage and disease.

Check Your Understanding

1. If *constricts* means to get smaller, what is the meaning of **dilate**?
   a. to get larger
   b. to open
   c. to get much smaller
   d. to not see
2. What are the floating objects you see in your eye if you look upwards and sideways?
   a. dust
   b. microscopic particles
   c. water
   d. smog
3. What is the main idea of the passage?
   a. The human eye is a remarkable organ of sight.
   b. The retina is sensitive to light.
   c. Blinking is harmful to the eye.
   d. Eye muscles move very often in one day.
4. What carries messages from the eye to the brain?
   a. the lens
   b. the retina
   c. nerves
   d. the cornea

/4

Name ______________________________

Warm-Up 29

Goblin Sharks

If your average sharks are scary enough, imagine how you might feel if you were to meet a goblin shark as you were swimming along. Their color is enough to startle any swimmer. They are bright bubblegum pink and range from three to thirteen feet long. The skin is softer and flabbier than most sharks. The goblin shark has a very long, triangular snout that looks like a large, pink triangular blade slicing through the water. This snout also helps the shark use its sixth sense to find prey. Sharks are able to sense electrical impulses given off by prey swimming in the surrounding water.

Like most sharks, this pink **predator** has very sharp teeth in the front of its mouth for grasping prey. It has smaller teeth in the back of its mouth for crunching bones and chewing flesh. Goblin sharks feed on fish, squid, crabs, lobsters, and other similar prey. When hunting, goblin sharks can even stick their jaws right out of their heads making them look even more ugly and terrifying. They use this extended jaw to catch prey. The strange pink color and scary appearance probably led to their name. They certainly look like truly scary Halloween creatures dreamed up by a horror movie writer. However, goblin sharks actually belong to a family of sharks known as mackerel sharks.

Check Your Understanding

1. From the context of the passage, what is the meaning of **predator**?
   a. an animal eaten by other animals
   b. man
   c. an animal that hunts other animals
   b. a plant-eating animal

2. Which word refers to the projecting nose and jaws of an animal?
   a. predator
   b. prey
   c. snout
   d. mouth

3. What is a shark's sixth sense?
   a. the ability to swim long distances
   b. the ability to sense electrical impulses from other living creatures
   c. the ability to thrust its jaw forward
   d. the ability to change colors

4. From the context of the passage, which is the best antonym for **predator**?
   a. snout
   b. hunter
   c. prey
   d. food

/4

Warm-Up 30

Name ____________________

A Plant Larger Than a Whale

One of the world's largest living organisms is not an elephant, a giant redwood tree, or a blue whale. The blue whale is the largest mammal on Earth and can weigh over 190 tons, but a 6,000-ton plant is more than thirty times heavier. This giant tree has more than 47,000 **Quaking** Aspen stems growing on a single root system. The plant is located in the mountains south of Utah. The stems look like separate trees. However, they are different stems of the same tree and form one single separate plant. The tree is the result of a natural process that created one single individual tree in what looks like a grove of trees. Every leaf in the entire plant is the same size, shape, and color. Individual stems may die, but the entire plant has survived for many years.

Quaking Aspens are the most common trees on the continent. The name "Quaking Aspen" refers to the nearly round leaves that appear to tremble or quake in the very slightest breeze. It is often the first tree to grow back after a fire or in forests where trees have been cut down. Aspen trees are used to make boxes, matches, furniture, and lumber used for building. Elk, moose, deer, beavers, rabbits, and other mammals feed on the twigs, leaves, buds, or bark. As a forest develops, aspens are often replaced by fir trees.

Check Your Understanding

1. Which of the following is an organism?
   a. an aspen tree
   b. a human being
   c. a blue whale
   d. all of the above
2. Which of the following has the same meaning as **quaking**?
   a. breaking
   b. barking
   c. trembling
   d. flying
3. What is the topic sentence in paragraph two?
   a. the second sentence
   b. the last sentence
   c. the first sentence
   d. none of the above
4. Why is the Quaking Aspen considered a single organism?
   a. It has a single root system.
   b. It has stems and leaves.
   c. All aspens are a single organism.
   d. All forests are one organism.

/4

From the Past

Warm-Up 1

Name ____________________

She Was Dressed to Meet an Iceberg

Molly Brown was a country girl who traveled to Colorado in the 1880s. She found work as a singer in a concert hall. Molly married a local miner named J. J. Brown who struck it rich mining silver. The couple built a huge house in Denver, Colorado. While J. J. went back to the minefields, Molly tried to make friends with other wealthy women. However, they considered her an ignorant country girl with poor speech and manners. She took a trip to Europe by herself in the hope of getting accepted by women in high society.

Molly's return trip to America was aboard the first voyage of the *Titanic*. It was interrupted when the ship struck an iceberg and started to sink. The new ocean liner was supposed to be unsinkable, but it quickly started to fill with water. Molly helped load women and children into one of the lifeboats. The rich women were dressed for dancing and dinner. Molly was wearing a huge fur coat. It was perfect for sitting on the ocean next to an iceberg. The people in the lifeboat, Molly included, were trying to escape from a sinking ship.

Molly used her coat as a blanket to cover cold and shivering women and children. Molly is said to have pulled out a cowboy pistol when the passengers were afraid and the crew was unwilling to row. They quickly decided to calm down and row. Molly herself helped row the boat to keep away from the sinking ship. Her courage and spirit made her a **heroine** on two continents. However, despite all her good deeds, she was never accepted by wealthy women.

Check Your Understanding

1. From the context of the passage, what is the meaning of **heroine**?
   a. male hero
   b. wealthy person
   c. female hero
   d. cowgirl

2. From the context of the passage, what is "high society"?
   a. a group of wealthy people who have been rich a long time
   b. a group of miners
   c. people who own boats
   d. people who have just become rich

3. Why did the frightened crew start to row the lifeboat?
   a. They were bored with sitting there.
   b. They wanted to go back to England.
   c. Molly pulled out a pistol.
   d. Molly offered them money.

4. According to the passage, why did Molly go to Europe?
   a. She was bored and wanted to learn to read.
   b. Molly wanted to be accepted by other wealthy women.
   c. She liked fine art and music.
   d. Her husband was mining, and she wanted to spend some money.

/4

Warm-Up 2

Name ______________________________

The Female Paul Revere

Paul Revere began his famous ride on the 18th of April in 1775. Sybil Ludington made hers on the 26th of April in 1777. The American Revolution had begun, and the British were trying to end the rebellion. Sybil's father led **volunteer militia** living in a large area in western New York. Sybil was his high-spirited sixteen-year-old daughter and the oldest of twelve children. The family was informed that British troops intended to burn a nearby town. She offered to ride out and alert her father's troops in their homes. The soldiers were to gather at her father's home, ready to defend the town.

Sybil took to her horse at 9:00 p.m. and rode all night until daybreak. She traveled through the dark, stormy night on a forty-mile route. She rode through many small neighboring towns. In villages and at lonely farmhouses, this brave girl woke up her father's citizen soldiers. She told them of the burning town. She could see the flames as she rode along on part of her route. Sybil was exhausted from her ride and from a fight with a thief who tried to rob her. She returned home drenched to the skin, but she was successful in alerting the four hundred men of her father's command. Her night ride was twice the distance of Paul Revere's. Although the town was burned, Sybil's courage was admired by many people. These included her father's men, her neighbors, and her father's commander, General George Washington. And don't forget, Sybil was just a teenager!

Check Your Understanding

1. How many years later than Paul Revere did Sybil Ludington make her ride?

a. about ten years
b. about one year
c. about two years
d. about twelve years

2. What problems did Sybil encounter on her ride?

a. She was attacked by a thief.
b. Her horse ran away.
c. The weather was wet and stormy.
d. both a and c

3. From the context of the passage, what is the best meaning of **volunteer militia**?

a. farmers
b. professional soldiers
c. firemen
d. soldiers from the local communities

4. Which event occurred second?

a. Sybil rides to warn the volunteer militia.
b. Sybil is honored for her courage during the ride.
c. Sybil's family is warned that the British intend to burn a local town.
d. Sybil fights off a thief.

/4

Warm-Up **3**

Name ______________________________

He Loved His Mother

The year was 1920 and Harry Burn, a twenty-four-year-old member of the Tennessee **legislature**, had a problem. There was an issue that was facing the nation. It was the much-debated question of the right of women to vote. For more than eighty years, women who wanted the right to vote had pressured leaders in the nation. The idea now had the support of most women and some men. Congress had voted. They decided to send a constitutional amendment to the legislatures. It was up to the forty-eight states to approve it.

If the legislatures of thirty-six states did not agree to the amendment, many men in the country could breathe easily. They thought the issue might go away. Harry Burn's problem was that thirty-five states had already approved the change. The only state remaining where the amendment had any chance was Tennessee. The Tennessee lawmakers split evenly at forty-eight in favor and forty-eight against. Harry's was the last undecided vote. Harry himself didn't much **favor** the idea of women voting. However, his mother had written him a letter begging him to "be a good boy." She wanted him to approve the new law.

After much soul searching, Harry Burn cast his vote in favor of the bill. Tennessee became the thirty-sixth state to approve the change. The right of women to vote was now the law of the land. Harry truly proved his love for his mother on this day.

Check Your Understanding

1. From the context of the passage, what is the best synonym for **favor**?
   a. reject
   b. approve
   c. debate
   d. decide
2. What would have happened to the amendment if Harry Burn had *not* voted to approve it?
   a. It would have passed anyway.
   b. The idea of women's suffrage would be forgotten.
   c. Some other state would have passed the amendment.
   d. The amendment would have failed, and women would not have had the right to vote at that time.
3. Which of the following is a fact and *not* an opinion?
   a. Everybody should have the right to vote.
   b. Only tall people should have the right to vote.
   c. The amendment gave women the right to vote.
   d. Men's votes are more important than women's votes.
4. From the context of the passage, what is the meaning of **legislature**?
   a. a place where laws are made
   b. a place where women vote
   c. a kind of law
   d. a job in Tennessee

/4

Warm-Up 4

Name ______________________________

The Rosetta Stone

One of the first written languages came from the very old societies of Egypt. This Egyptian writing is called **hieroglyphics**. These were symbols carved on stone buildings or statues. They were sometimes written on a kind of paper made from reeds. Over time, the symbols for simple objects, such as spears or buildings, slowly changed to symbols for words. This change allowed more detailed ideas to be expressed in writing. The problem was that the actual meaning of the words carved on tombs and other buildings from long ago could not be read later, even by experts in languages. A few pictures sometimes seemed obvious in their meaning. Nobody knew how the language was organized. They could only guess at the meanings of most of the words and pictures.

The discovery of the Rosetta Stone in 1799 by a French army officer changed the situation. The stone was found in the Nile Delta. This stone led to an understanding of this ancient Egyptian writing. The stone was carved with a copy of an order announcing a new Egyptian ruler. The stone was partly damaged, but the writing was clear enough to be seen. The stone recorded the same message in three different languages. One was in hieroglyphics. One was written in a simpler form of the same language, and one was in Greek. Because ancient Greek was a language known to scholars, the two other languages could then be decoded. In 1822, a French expert in languages **decoded** both Egyptian languages. This breakthrough made it possible to read the words on other tombs, buildings, and papers written by ancient Egyptians.

Check Your Understanding

1. From the context of the passage, what is the best meaning of **hieroglyphics**?
   a. Egyptian writing using symbols and pictures
   b. ancient Greek
   c. stone writing
   d. old English writing

2. From the context of the passage, what is the meaning of **decoded**?
   a. to look at a language
   b. to write the language
   c. to translate the language into another language
   d. to write a new language

3. From the context of the passage, what is the Rosetta Stone?
   a. a rock with writing in three languages
   b. a kind of Greek language
   c. a form of simplified hieroglyphics
   d. a French stone

4. What was the most important effect of the discovery of the Rosetta Stone?
   a. Egyptian hieroglyphics were translated.
   b. People learned to speak modern Egyptian languages.
   c. Ancient Greek could now be translated.
   d. all of the above

/4

Warm-Up 5

Name ______________________________

The Mausoleum of Halicarnassus

About 2,400 years ago, Halicarnassus was the leading city in a small kingdom called Caria. It was located in what is now the nation of Turkey. King Mausolus ruled over the area for about twenty years. He had a rather quiet and unimportant reign. It was marked by only two interesting events—his marriage to his sister and his death. It was common in Caria and other places in the ancient world for leaders to marry their sisters. This made it possible for them to keep power and wealth in the family. Artemisia, the king's wife, truly loved and even adored her husband. When the king died, she decided to build a tomb for him as a great honor to his memory. The Mausoleum of Halicarnassus was the result. It was considered one of the seven wonders of the ancient world.

The queen hired the best sculptors, designers, and builders from Greece. They built a marble tomb about 100 feet square and 140 feet high. It included a row of thirty-six columns. There was a twenty-four-step pyramid. A marble chariot with four horses sat at the top. There were dozens of beautifully carved statues around the temple. There were many detailed and colorful carvings of battles.

The building was actually finished after the death of the queen. She died two years after her husband and was buried in the same tomb. Their monument survived for more than 1,700 years. A series of earthquakes destroyed the building about 600 years ago. The word *mausoleum* has entered the language as a word meaning "large tomb."

Check Your Understanding

1. Who was Artemisia?
   a. the wife of King Mausolus
   b. the sister of Mausolus
   c. a person entombed in the mausoleum
   d. all of the above
2. How many years did the mausoleum survive?
   a. nearly 17 years
   b. more than 1,700 years
   c. more than 2,300 years
   d. about 600 years
3. From the context of the passage, what is a mausoleum used for?
   a. a temple
   b. a large burial tomb
   c. a palace
   d. a place to display sculptures
4. Which of the following is an opinion and *not* a fact?
   a. King Mausolus was entombed about 2,350 years ago.
   b. King Mausolus was married to his sister.
   c. An earthquake destroyed the Mausoleum at Halicarnassus.
   d. King Mausolus was a great leader.

/4

Warm-Up 6

Name ______________________________

The Invention of Basketball

Most sports don't have a specific date or place where they were invented. They often developed over many years from child's play or community games. Basketball, however, was invented in December 1891 by Dr. James Naismith. He was a physical education teacher at a school that is now known as Springfield College in Massachusetts. He believed that there needed to be an indoor game that could be played in the evenings and during the cold, snowy months of winter. Football was too rough to play inside. In addition, the offense in football could run with the ball. This required the defense to tackle and play rough. Football was a very dangerous college sport before the invention of modern protections, such as helmets and pads. Many college players were killed or badly hurt in the early years of football. However, the basic idea of basketball is that it is to be played with skill rather than roughness.

The **original** game used seven men on each side and two peach baskets into which a ball was shot. The early game quickly became popular with college students. Oftentimes, there were many players on each side. The ball could not be kicked or carried. If a basket was made by one side, "time" was called while the ball was taken out of the basket by a coach or player with a ladder. By 1897, the game had changed, and five players were on each side. By 1912, the modern hoop, made of net with an open bottom, had replaced the peach baskets. Dr. Naismith laid out thirteen original rules for the game. Twelve of the rules are still used in the game today.

Check Your Understanding

1. Which was *not* a reason for the invention of basketball?
   a. Football was too rough and dangerous.
   b. Basketball could be played indoors in cold weather.
   c. Tall athletes needed a game to favor them.
   d. Students needed safe, energetic exercise.

2. What can you infer was the reason peach baskets were replaced with hoops?
   a. The players didn't have ladders.
   b. Stopping to retrieve the ball after a basket was made slowed down the game too much.
   c. There were too many players in some games.
   d. There weren't enough peach baskets.

3. From the context of the passage, what is the best meaning of **original**?
   a. invented
   b. developed gradually
   c. the beginning or the first of something
   d. a copy of something

4. How do you know that the basic idea of basketball has *not* changed?
   a. Nearly all of the basic rules have stayed the same.
   b. You still may not carry the ball.
   c. It still uses a peach basket.
   d. both a and b

/4

Warm-Up 7

Name ______________________________

Laura Ingalls Wilder: Pioneer Author

In 1930, a daughter of pioneers decided to write the story of her frontier life. She was sixty-seven years old. She wanted schoolchildren to understand how people lived during America's early days. In her first book, Laura Ingalls Wilder describes life growing up in a log cabin in the woods. The book was a great success. Wilder went on to publish seven more *Little House* books.

Wilder describes moving west in a covered wagon, as well as her life on the prairie. She describes living in a sod house on the plains. Wilder tells of thousands of hungry grasshoppers destroying their crops. She recalls the bitter cold winter on the plains. She helped her father twist hay to use as fuel for their fire because there was no wood to burn. The **author** describes her father's job building a railroad across the plains. Wilder painfully remembers her sister Mary's fever, which led to her blindness. She recalls her own work sewing buttons in a store. *These Happy Golden Years* describes her experiences as a young schoolteacher in a one-room schoolhouse. Wilder even describes her own romance with the young man who became her husband. *Farmer Boy* tells the story of his boyhood on a farm.

Wilder's words paint a true picture of pioneer life on the frontier. They tell of the simple joys of family activities. They help readers experience education in a small country school. They record the heartbreaking pain and the dangers of the frontier. Each of her stories explains the sacrifices made by people who wanted to own their own land and home. Her books celebrate the pioneer spirit, which is an important part of America's history.

Check Your Understanding

1. From the context of the passage, which is the best synonym for **author**?
   a. writer
   b. artist
   c. teacher
   d. actor
2. Why did Laura and her father twist hay?
   a. They fed it to the cows this way.
   b. They burned it for heat.
   c. They used it to keep their beds warm.
   d. They wanted to store it for the summer.
3. Which of the following did Wilder describe about her life?
   a. life on a farm in the woods
   b. life in a prairie home
   c. life on the plains
   d. all of the above
4. Which of the following is an opinion and *not* a fact?
   a. Wilder wrote her stories in longhand.
   b. Wilder's daughter typed her manuscripts.
   c. Wilder wrote interesting stories.
   d. Wilder's stories were about her own life.

/4

Warm-Up 8

Name ______________________________

Food on the *Mayflower*

On September 6, 1620, a group of 102 passengers, including the Pilgrims and a few other families, set out from England to cross the Atlantic Ocean. They sailed on a crowded wooden ship called the *Mayflower*. The voyage took sixty-six days to reach the shore of what is now Massachusetts. The passengers slept and ate while crowded together in the main cabin. They rarely washed their hands and never bathed or changed their clothes. Their hair and clothes were covered with lice, fleas, and roaches. They also brought along farm animals, which added to the smell and filth of the voyage.

The travelers ate moldy green cheese, dried peas, salty beef, and dried fish. They fought to keep the mice and rats on the ship away from these foods. They sucked on rock-hard biscuits to make them soft enough to swallow. The biscuits often had tunnels in them made by maggots. The voyagers also ate dried vegetables, such as turnips, parsnips, onions, and cabbages. One of their favorite foods was dried ox tongue.

The travelers used some spices, such as ginger and cloves, to cover up the taste of spoiled food. To overcome the salty taste, they drank beer, wine, and ale. Even the children drank these! Clean, fresh water was seldom available. On a few rare occasions, passengers were able to use fireboxes to make soup, dumplings, and oatmeal. Life aboard the *Mayflower* was no "picnic," but all hoped for a better life in the new world.

Check Your Understanding

1. Which of these was *not* a problem faced by the voyagers on the *Mayflower*?
   a. The food was very salty and often spoiled.
   b. The rats and insects got into their food.
   c. They didn't have much fresh water.
   d. They didn't have spices to season their food.

2. Where might the passengers have found fresh water?
   a. in barrels on the ship
   b. from rain falling on the ship during storms
   c. from the Atlantic Ocean
   d. in a refrigerator

3. What is the main idea of the passage?
   a. The *Mayflower* passengers had a good trip to the new world.
   b. The food on the *Mayflower* was not very pleasant to eat, but there was enough to survive on.
   c. The *Mayflower* was a pleasure cruise for rich travelers.
   d. There were 102 passengers.

4. From the context of the passage, what can you infer about the children on the *Mayflower*?
   a. They made many sacrifices during the voyage.
   b. They were spoiled by their parents.
   c. They were better fed than adults.
   d. They were treated to tasty foods.

/4

Warm-Up **9**

Name ______________________________

The Library at Alexandria

The Library at Alexandria was founded by the rulers of Egypt. This was hundreds of years before the time of Christ. The library was the brain center of the ancient world. It held more written material than any other place on Earth at that time. Books were in the form of handwritten, rolled-up scrolls. Over the centuries, the rulers had copied, stolen, borrowed, and paid vast sums of money for these books. They had been collected throughout the world. These included the works of many different people and stories from many religions.

These handwritten works were very valuable and very expensive. More than half a million of these scrolls were stored in the library. These included writings in many languages.

But this library was not just a library. It was also a museum and learning center where many discoveries were made. In addition, it was a university where scholars from all over the world came to study. Many great thinkers, writers, and teachers studied there. The greatest woman teacher in the world at that time taught at the library.

Alexandria was the home of the library. It was a very active center of business and trade. People from many lands and cultures lived in this community. Unfortunately, the great library was damaged by mobs at different times. It was burned several times and finally left in ruins.

Check Your Understanding

1. What other functions were also served by the Library of Alexandria?

a. museum
b. marketplace
c. university
d. both a and c

2. From the context of the passage, what can you conclude about scrolls?

a. They were expensive.
b. Scrolls were written in many languages.
c. They came from many cultures.
d. all of the above

3. Books in the library collection were published in the form of

a. flat pages.
b. rolled-up, handwritten scrolls.
c. CDs.
d. electronic books.

4. What happened to the library?

a. It was burned several times.
b. It ran out of books.
c. The city closed the library.
d. both a and c

/4

Warm-Up 10

Name ______________________

John Adams Defends British Soldiers

In 1768, England sent troops to Boston to help collect taxes on tea, glass, paint, lead, and paper. They were ordered to guard the building where taxes were collected. On March 5, 1770, a loud and angry mob of sailors and workingmen rioted in front of that building. The soldiers opened fire only after they were insulted, hit with snowballs, and threatened with violence. Five men in the mob were killed, and six others were injured. The colonists were very angry. They called it a **massacre**, even though only a few rioters were killed.

No lawyer in the city wanted to anger his fellow citizens by defending the soldiers. John Adams was a lawyer who opposed the new taxes. However, he accepted the job because he believed that every citizen had a right to a fair trial. He felt this included the soldiers who were only following orders. Adams told the jury that the soldiers were endangered by the mob. Therefore, they had a right to shoot in order to defend themselves.

The officer in charge was found innocent. The jury didn't believe he ordered his men to fire on the mob. Adams even got the two soldiers who were found guilty of murder free because of a strange loophole in the law. All he had to prove was that the men could read. He was able to prove this, and they were freed. John Adams went on to become a leader in the struggle for America's freedom from England.

Check Your Understanding

1. From the context of the passage, what can be inferred about the character of John Adams?
   a. He wanted to make money.
   b. He was a dedicated and capable lawyer.
   c. He wanted people to pay their taxes.
   d. He wanted to be a judge.
2. Why did John Adams defend the unpopular British soldiers?
   a. He received a large fee from the British.
   b. He wanted to run for public office.
   c. He thought the soldiers were entitled to fire on the citizens.
   d. He thought all citizens were entitled to a fair trial.
3. Which of the following best describes the meaning of **massacre**?
   a. a snowball fight
   b. the killing of many people
   c. a murder
   d. a riot
4. Which terms best describe the character and personality of John Adams?
   a. honorable and clever
   b. devious and mean
   c. angry and cruel
   d. tricky and cheap

/4

Warm-Up 11

Name ______________________________

The Travels of Marco Polo

In 1271, Marco Polo, a seventeen-year-old teenager, traveled with his father and uncle on a journey to China. They went to the court of Kublai Khan. The journey took three and a half years. It was filled with dangers, including bandits and bad weather. The men traveled through blazing hot sand and wild lands. They crossed high mountains and a huge desert. Marco kept careful journals of all that he saw and many of the stories he heard.

After his return, Marco talked to a writer about his journey. He described things people had never seen or heard about. His story was published as *The Travels of Marco Polo.* He described great palaces, rich princes, and things never experienced in Europe. He said that he had seen burning rocks, which we call coal today. He told of oil seeping from the ground. He said it was used for lighting and medicine. He explained the use of paper money in China long before other nations used this kind of money. Marco explained how the Great Khan kept his empire united under his control by using a fast mail system. Letters and orders were sent by a pony express across the kingdom. Marco talked of gold-covered temples and kings with piles of pearls and rubies. He described the rhinoceros and crocodile among other animals new to Europe. The long-time traveler told many tales of the people he met and their customs.

The Polos were finally allowed to leave China as **ambassadors** for the Khan. They delivered a princess from the Khan as a bride for a king. Many readers thought Marco's stories were made up, but most of the things Marco Polo said he saw have been proven to be true.

Check Your Understanding

1. From the context of the passage, what are **ambassadors**?
   a. people who represent a king or a country
   b. writers of fairy tales
   c. rich men
   d. noblemen

2. What dangers did the Polos encounter on their trip to China?
   a. robbers
   b. bad weather and hot deserts
   c. high mountains
   d. all of the above

3. From the context of the passage, what can you infer about the tales Marco told?
   a. The stories were entirely made up.
   b. Marco Polo was angry at Kublai Khan.
   c. The stories told by Marco were very likely true.
   d. Marco Polo never went to China.

4. Which event occurred first?
   a. Marco Polo returned to Venice.
   b. Marco traveled over many mountains to reach China.
   c. The Polos delivered a princess to a king.
   d. Marco kept a journal of his travels.

/4

Warm-Up
12

Name ____________________

An Unusual Pharaoh

Akhenaten came to power as the pharaoh of Egypt about 3,340 years ago and ruled for nearly eighteen years. He was an unusual leader. He created a lot of anger and distrust among the priests, leaders, and common people of his land. He was not like the other rulers before him. He did not spend his time trying to please all of the many gods of his country's religion. He was **devoted** only to a less important god known as Aten, the sun god. The symbol of this god was a sun on a round disk without a face. The circle was sitting high in the sky. This god did not have very many myths, stories, and beliefs about him. Many other gods had more stories and more people who worshipped them.

Akhenaten and his wife were determined to change the religion to worship this one god instead of the many gods. The pharaoh was the top religious leader in the land. Many of his subjects and most of the priests felt that he was putting the nation in danger by making all of the other gods angry. However, the determined king built a new capital city dedicated to Aten. He and his wife were very determined to change the minds of his people.

How Akhenaten died is a mystery. Some historians think he may have been killed by enemies who disliked his new city and new religion. Others think he may have died of illness or some other natural cause. After his death, the next ruler and the priests quickly returned to the old capital city and the old religious practices. Akhenaten was the father of King Tut, who died at a young age.

Check Your Understanding

1. Which of the following would be the best title for the passage?
- a. "Gods and Pharaohs"
- b. "Aten's Pharaoh"
- c. "High in the Sky"
- d. "The Mysterious Death"

2. From the context of the passage, who would most likely be referred to as **devoted**?
- a. a friend
- b. a leader
- c. a believer and follower
- d. a king

3. What would a determined ruler be likely to do?
- a. do exactly what his predecessors did
- b. do things his own way, regardless of criticism
- c. look for fights
- d. do what is expected of him

4. According to the passage, who was related to Akhenaten?
- a. King Tut
- b. a Greek queen
- c. Aten
- d. both a and b

/4

Warm-Up 13

Name ______________________

A Number Challenge

Suppose your teacher gave you an assignment to add all of the numbers from 1 to 100 without using a calculator. How long do you think it would take? You could do it in about 30 seconds.

Here's how: Add 1 plus 100, which equals 101. Add 2 plus 99, which equals 101. Add 3 plus 98, which also equals 101. You are adding 50 pairs of numbers, which all equal 101. Therefore, you can multiply 50 times 101. This equals 5,050. Multiplication, of course, is simply a fast method of addition when you use the same numbers.

The mathematician who worked out this particular problem was named Carl Gauss. He lived from 1777 to 1855. As a college student, he discovered that a seventeen-sided figure could be drawn with just a compass and a ruler. This was thought to be impossible.

During his lifetime, Gauss made many discoveries in the study of numbers and shapes. He studied the use of statistics. This is the science of collecting, using, and studying information from real events in life. Gauss also studied stars and planets. He became famous for discovering the orbit around the sun of the asteroid Ceres. See if you can add all the numbers from 1 to 100 in less than 30 seconds! Maybe you, too, will become a scientist or math expert!

Check Your Understanding

1. Which of the following is an example of statistics?
   a. determining World Series scores since 1920
   b. estimating barrels of oil sold by a company in a year
   c. figuring out grades a student gets over the course of a year
   d. all of the above

2. From the context of the passage, what can you infer about Ceres?
   a. No one had known about its orbit until Gauss.
   b. Ceres is a part of our solar system.
   c. Ceres travels through a solar system and never returns.
   d. both a and b

3. Which word in the passage refers to "the study and use of numbers"?
   a. astronomy
   b. data
   c. physics
   d. statistics

4. Which number would be added to 91 in the pattern described in the first paragraph?
   a. 0
   b. 21
   c. 10
   d. any number

/4

Warm-Up 14

Name ______________________________

The History of the Book

The first writing began with the Sumerians about 5,500 years ago. It was done on rectangular clay blocks. Most of the time this writing contained lists of materials or words. Writing in Egyptian symbols was done on papyrus about 5,000 years ago. Papyrus was made from reeds that grew in the water. These sheets of papyrus were rolled around wooden poles. Several **scrolls** of this type made a book. Later, smaller rolls of papyrus were used. They could be unwound and studied.

The Greeks got their papyrus from a port city called Byblos. They used rolls of papyrus, but they also developed the idea of folding papyrus leaves together and binding them with a kind of string or thread. They used the name of the port, Byblos, for these bound sheets of folded paper. The word *bible*, meaning "book," has come to us through that city's name.

People in northern India wrote on sheets of birch bark and collected written sheets in wooden boxes. The Chinese used bamboo tablets until about 2,200 years ago when they developed scrolls made of the by-products of silk production. Some Middle Easterners wrote on animal skins. This leather parchment was invented about 2,165 years ago. The sheets were folded to look somewhat like our modern books.

The invention of the printing press changed books forever. No longer did books need to be written by hand. The folded sheets attached within a hard cover changed life for all readers.

Check Your Understanding

1. Which of these materials served as a form of paper?
   a. papyrus
   b. parchment
   c. birch bark
   d. all of the above

2. From the context of the passage, what is a **scroll**?
   a. a dessert
   b. a kind of book rolled around a cylinder
   c. a port
   d. a printing press

3. Which of these phrases best describes a modern book?
   a. a scroll
   b. birch bark
   c. folded sheets attached within a durable cover
   d. a printing press

4. From the context of the passage, what can you infer about all ancient books?
   a. They were all written on papyrus.
   b. They were inexpensive.
   c. They were harder to use.
   d. all of the above

/4

Name ____

Warm-Up
15

Female Pirates

Women were rarely allowed on pirate ships, except when they were captured from other ships. They became part of the stolen treasure of gold, food, and weapons. A few women did choose to become pirates. They usually pretended they were men by dressing in men's clothes and fighting with swords and pistols just like male pirates. Some were even married to male pirates.

A Swedish princess ran away from an unhappy marriage and became a pirate more than twelve hundred years ago. Grace O'Malley, an Irish lady from a noble family, had her own fleet of pirate galleys propelled by oars and sails. She attacked many treasure ships sailing in the Atlantic Ocean in the 1500s. She lived a long life and died at the advanced age of seventy-three.

Two of the most famous female pirates sailed on John "Calico Jack" Rackham's ship. Mary Read had been serving in the British army as a soldier when her ship was captured by Rackham. She promptly joined his crew and became famous as a ferocious pirate warrior. Mary was an expert with the cutlass (a short, thick, curved sword). She also fought sword duels with fellow pirates when she was angry. Anne Bonny, on the same ship, left her husband to join Rackham. She carried a short ax, two pistols, and a sword. Both women were sentenced to hang when their ship was captured by the British navy. Mary died of illness in jail, and Anne disappeared after she was pardoned by the authorities. A pirate's life may have been full of adventure, but it didn't always end that way.

Check Your Understanding

1. Which of the female pirates had served as a British soldier?
   a. Anne Bonny
   b. Mary Read
   c. Grace O'Malley
   d. Alwilda
2. Which of the following is the best summary of the passage?
   a. Mary Read and Anne Bonny were successful pirates.
   b. Female pirates were rare but interesting people.
   c. No female pirate was ever captured.
   d. Female pirates didn't know how to fight.
3. Which of these sentences is an opinion and *not* a fact?
   a. There were some female pirates.
   b. Women did not make good pirates.
   c. Female pirates sometimes dressed in men's clothing.
   d. Some female pirates fought sword duels when they were angry.
4. Which word refers to "a ship propelled by oars and sails"?
   a. cruiser
   b. cutlass
   c. galley
   d. fleet

/4

Warm-Up 16

Name ______________________________

Kites

Kites are among the oldest inventions (and **toys**) of humankind. They have been around for at least 3,000 years since their invention in China. Although they have always been playthings for children and adults, they have been used for more serious purposes, as well. In China and some other Asian countries, kites have been used for fishing. Instead of just using a fishing pole, the fisherman flies a kite far out over the water with a fishing line, hook, and sinker dangling from the kite. When a fish bites, the kite is jerked upward by the kite-flying fisherman. The fish becomes airborne and then is pulled in as the kite is brought back to shore. Flying kites at night to ward off evil spirits is also a practice that dates back to ancient times in China. Kites have been used as signaling devices for armies and for ships. A few were built to support a person who was carried as a spy flying over the army of an enemy.

The inventor of the telephone, Alexander Graham Bell, created a new kind of kite, the tetrahedral kite. It is made of four triangular sides. Bell used very light balsa wood to make his kites. He even designed a boat in the same triangular shape to pull his huge kites. He was able to carry a 220-pound man on the kite that he pulled into the air using the boat. Kites are still popular playthings in many parts of the world for children of all ages with their eyes on the skies. When is the last time you flew a kite?

Check Your Understanding

1. Which word in the passage means "a flying object"?
a. tetrahedral
b. balsa
c. ancient
d. airborne

2. How many sides are on a tetrahedron?
a. one
b. two
c. four
d. six

3. Which is the best topic sentence in the passage?
a. paragraph one, last sentence
b. paragraph two, last sentence
c. paragraph one, first sentence
d. paragraph two, first sentence

4. From the context of the passage, which is a synonym for **toys**?
a. playthings
b. dangling
c. flying
d. balsa

/4

Warm-Up 17

Name ______________________________

Presidential Pets

Like the people they represent, American presidents and their families have been fond of pets. John Quincy Adams once kept an alligator in the White House for several months. It belonged to a visiting French hero. His wife kept much calmer company. She raised silkworms and fed them mulberry leaves. Abraham Lincoln's family kept rabbits and two goats.

Franklin D. Roosevelt liked dogs. He grew up surrounded by them. After spending seven years in the White House, the president was given a dog as a gift. It was a Scottie that he nicknamed Fala. The president made Fala famous in one of his speeches. The Secret Service called Fala "The Informer" because when it was seen on secret trips, people knew the president was nearby. President Coolidge's office was home to a raccoon named Rebecca. He also kept a wallaby, a black bear, lion cubs, and thirteen Pekin ducks. William Henry Harrison kept both a cow and a billy goat. Thomas Jefferson loved his pet mockingbird. President Taft kept a cow on the White House lawn.

The champion pet keepers were the family of Theodore Roosevelt. At one time or another, they had a badger and five bears, including a cub that was the model for the original "teddy bear." They also kept a lion, a hyena, a wildcat, a barn owl, various snakes and lizards, a coyote, a pony, and a zebra. It takes a lot to entertain six children!

Check Your Understanding

1. Which president mentioned his dog in a speech?
   a. Theodore Roosevelt
   b. Franklin D. Roosevelt
   c. John Quincy Adams
   d. Abraham Lincoln

2. Which presidential family had the widest variety of pets?
   a. Abraham Lincoln
   b. Franklin D. Roosevelt
   c. Calvin Coolidge
   d. Theodore Roosevelt

3. Which president kept a pet for a visiting hero?
   a. John Quincy Adams
   b. George Washington
   c. William Howard Taft
   d. Abraham Lincoln

4. What is the author's purpose in writing the passage?
   a. to inform the reader
   b. to amuse the reader
   c. to explain politics to the reader
   d. both a and b

/4

Warm-Up 18 Name ____________________

The Iceman

One of the greatest discoveries in the study of man's history was the uncovering of the frozen body of a man in 1991. He was soon called "The Iceman." The body had been well **preserved** by ice in the glacier-covered Alps for about 5,300 years. The man lived in a period called the Copper Age. Among the possessions found with the hunter were a copper ax, flint arrowheads, a wooden bow, fourteen arrows in a leather quiver, and bark containers. He carried a pouch with mushrooms and a fungus. These were probably used for medicine. He wore a bearskin hat, a goatskin coat, leather shoes, and a belt. He also wore a grass cape that appears to have been warm and able to shed water during rain or snowstorms.

Scientists studying the body have determined that he was probably in his late 40s and was about 5 feet, 2 inches tall. The man had broken several bones in his life. He suffered from arthritis and his lungs were black from smoke. He would have inhaled smoke from cooking fires all of his life. The hunter had recently been shot in the left shoulder by an arrow, which probably caused his death. He had tattoos on his back, knees, ankles, and wrist. They were made from rubbing charcoal into small cuts in the skin. These may have had some tribal importance. They might have been related to a religious practice or been personal body decorations.

Check Your Understanding

1. From the context of the passage, what is the meaning of **preserved**?
   a. kept from decaying
   b. used for cooking
   c. to be afraid of animals
   d. dried in dirt

2. From the context of the passage, what can you infer a quiver is used for?
   a. a place to keep medicine
   b. a case used to hold arrows
   c. a way to stop trembling
   d. a piece of wood

3. Which of the following might a scientist conclude from a study of the Iceman and his belongings?
   a. People of his time knew how to use animal skins for clothing.
   b. Hunting was of major importance in the lives of these people.
   c. People suffered from wounds and diseases.
   d. all of the above

4. Which of the following facts would support the proposition that life was very dangerous for people in the time of the Iceman?
   a. The Iceman had several broken bones.
   b. The Iceman was wearing tattoos.
   c. The Iceman's last meal had included meat and wheat.
   d. The Iceman wore a bearskin hat.

/4

Warm-Up 19 Name ____________________

Attempted Presidential Assassinations

There have been several unsuccessful attempts to shoot presidents in the last two hundred years. In January 1835, an out-of-work house painter aimed a single-shot pistol at Andrew Jackson. The president was on his way to a funeral service. Luckily, the gun misfired. The sixty-seven-year-old former general charged his attacker who pulled another pistol and fired again. It too failed to fire. Jackson grabbed the would-be shooter and started hitting him. He had to be pulled away from the surprised gunman.

In 1912, Theodore Roosevelt was running for another four-year term as president. He was about to speak to a large group. An unknown man rushed out of the crowd and shot him in the chest at close range. The bullet **plowed** into the thick, folded speech Roosevelt had planned to deliver. It then hit his metal glasses case before it entered his chest. Although wounded and in pain, Roosevelt refused to go to the hospital until he had given his speech.

Two men tried to kill President Truman in a house where he was staying. One man was killed and the other was wounded by Secret Service agents. Truman was unhurt. Two mentally disturbed women tried to shoot President Ford. This was within seventeen days of each other in September 1975 in California. Both were arrested. Ford was not hurt. A mentally ill young man did wound President Reagan in 1981. Fortunately, Reagan **recovered** rapidly.

Check Your Understanding

1. From the context of the passage, what is the best meaning of **plowed**?
   a. to fall to the ground
   b. to bounce off
   c. to pass through
   d. to move forcefully through something
2. From the context of the passage, which is the best synonym for **recovered**?
   a. fell
   b. healed
   c. moved
   d. spoke
3. Which president was shot at the White House?
   a. Harry Truman
   b. Gerald Ford
   c. Theodore Roosevelt
   d. none of the presidents
4. Which piece of information supports the proposition that Andrew Jackson was courageous?
   a. Jackson attacked the would-be assassin.
   b. Jackson was on his way to a funeral service.
   c. Jackson owned a plantation.
   d. both a and b

/4

Warm-Up

Name ______________________________

20 America's Forgotten Warriors

Thousands of African Americans served in the Union army during the Civil War. Most of these soldiers went back home after the war. However, about 2,000 of them chose to join "colored" units. They were put together as groups of mounted soldiers. They learned to ride horses with skill. The units were sent to the frontier west of the Mississippi River. There, these horse soldiers protected the interests of the country and defended white settlers in that dangerous land. They planted telegraph poles and strung hundreds of miles of telegraph line. They defended railroad workers who were laying railroad tracks against American Indian attacks. The soldiers worked as lawmen in the wild open spaces. They captured outlaws and cattle thieves. They were not trained in mapmaking, and some could not read. However, they drew careful and detailed maps of large areas of the West. These maps drew people from the settled states to move west and build homes and farms.

The men were nicknamed "Buffalo Soldiers" as a sign of respect by the American Indians. These warriors recognized the soldiers' courage and skill. At the same time, these African American soldiers were often treated with disrespect by some of their white officers. They were also not respected by many white settlers. For thirty years, these soldiers helped provide the safety that led to the creation of eight western states. They rode thousands of miles in their duties. They fought in hundreds of battles against the native people of the West. These soldiers suffered heavy losses in dead and wounded men. However, they were seldom honored by their country for their service or their courage.

Check Your Understanding

1. Who nicknamed the African Americans as "Buffalo Soldiers"?
   a. the general in charge
   b. African American soldiers
   c. white settlers
   d. American Indians

2. Where did the soldiers serve?
   a. east of the Mississippi River
   b. west of the Mississippi River
   c. Canada
   d. New York

3. Which word refers to "wounded and killed soldiers"?
   a. losses
   b. natives
   c. officers
   d. settlers

4. Which statement can you infer is true?
   a. White settlers and leaders always appreciated the Buffalo Soldiers.
   b. The American Indians didn't respect the fighting ability of the Buffalo Soldiers.
   c. There was mutual respect between many Buffalo Soldiers and American Indians.
   d. The soldiers had black officers.

/4

Warm-Up 21

Name ________________________________

The First Great Emperor

In the year 221 BCE, the first great emperor of China united the nation and became the complete master of his kingdom. He called himself Qin Shi Huang (Chin Shee Whang). He was a tireless ruler, but he trusted no one. Qin created a new capital city for China. He created a single money system to be used by all of his **subjects** in all of China. He started a single, unified system of weights and measurements for everything. This even included the size of cartwheels.

Qin forced thousands of his subjects to work on his special projects. His most famous project is still visible today. He began building the 5,500-mile long Great Wall of China. The Great Wall cost so many lives that it was called "the longest graveyard in the world." He also insisted on digging canals, building new forts, and fixing old roads. This emperor trusted no one. He even ordered the destruction of most of the books in the kingdom. These books included those of the great Chinese philosopher, Confucius. Many scholars buried their books to save them. However, if the king's servants found the buried or hidden books, the owners were killed on the spot.

One of the emperor's most secret projects was discovered in modern China. In 1974, a farmer accidentally fell into an underground tomb where he found an entire army standing in order. The army was made of terra cotta, a kind of clay. The emperor had more than 8,000 of these clay figures in his tomb. These included warriors, chariots, and horses. Surprisingly, scientists believe that there are even more of these clay figures that have yet to be discovered.

Check Your Understanding

1. Which word refers to a kind of clay?
   a. realm
   b. visible
   c. terra cotta
   d. executed
2. From the context of the passage, what can you infer from the description of the Great Wall of China?
   a. The wall was very long.
   b. Many workers died during its construction.
   c. It was used as a cemetery.
   d. Workers liked building the wall.
3. What was the effect of the emperor's orders to destroy books?
   a. Scholars took great risks to save their books.
   b. Many writings of Confucius were destroyed.
   c. Some books were hidden underground.
   d. all of the above
4. From the context of the passage, what is the best meaning of **subjects**?
   a. kingdom
   b. things a king studies
   c. books
   d. people ruled by a king or emperor

/4

Warm-Up 22

Name ______________________________

Lincoln's Man

Most people don't know this. President Lincoln paid a man to take his place as a soldier during the Civil War. The draft laws of that war allowed a wealthy man to pay another man to serve for him in the army. These men were either too old, ill, or unable to serve in the army. In 1864, Lincoln asked an assistant to find him a man of courage and honor to serve for him in the army.

His assistant happened to see John Staples walking along with his father on the streets of Washington. The assistant asked the young man, who was not yet twenty-one years old, if he would like to serve for Lincoln in the army. The man agreed, but his father had to give his approval, as well. The father soon agreed, and the young man was paid $500 for his service.

Staples had already served for another man earlier in the war when he was living in another state. After serving for a few months, he had become ill with a serious fever and had been discharged from the army in 1863.

Lincoln met Staples and his father, and he approved the choice. He told them that he hoped the young man would be one of the lucky ones. Staples rejoined the army on October 1, 1864, and served for a year. By then the war was over, and he returned to his home in Pennsylvania. Lincoln was shot a year later in April 1865. Staples died in 1888 of a heart attack at the age of forty-three. They are both remembered for their sacrifice and dedication.

Check Your Understanding

1. Why would Lincoln want to pay a substitute to serve in the army for him?
   a. As president of the United States, he should not put his life at risk.
   b. He was required to find someone.
   c. He wanted somebody who could shoot straight.
   d. He wanted to embarrass his enemies.

2. Which of the following is an opinion and *not* a fact?
   a. Lincoln wanted to set an example by hiring a substitute.
   b. The cost of paying a substitute was too high.
   c. Staples' father became a chaplain in his son's regiment.
   d. Staples was not twenty-one when he became Lincoln's substitute.

3. From the context of the passage, which word means "a selection of people for military service"?
   a. draft
   b. discharged
   c. substitute
   d. assistant

4. Why did John Staples leave the army in 1863?
   a. He had a heart attack.
   b. He had a serious fever.
   c. The war was over.
   d. He wasn't happy.

/4

Warm-Up 23

Name ______________________________

The First Ferris Wheel

The directors of the 1893 Chicago World's Fair needed something special to mark their event. The Eiffel Tower had been constructed for the Paris World's Fair in 1889. Architects and engineers made many proposals for towers, but they really didn't hold anybody's interest. A bridge builder and engineer named George Ferris had a different idea. He wanted to create a monster wheel 250 feet tall. It would be a moving wheel with spokes like a bicycle. He intended to carry more than 2,000 people on each ride. Altogether, they would weigh more than 200,000 pounds.

Ferris convinced a very doubtful committee to let him build the wheel at his own expense. He built his huge wheel and then cemented two giant towers into the earth to hold the wheel. The axle that would hold the giant wheel weighed about fifty tons. Two powerful engines could turn the wheel with a huge chain near the edge of the wheel. The spokes of the wheel would hold thirty-six large wooden boxes. Each box could hold sixty people. The maximum number of people on the ride at one time was 2,160 people. The giant boxes had five glass windows on each side, and iron grills kept people from falling out. The entire wheel was 250 feet across. To make night rides more **impressive**, Ferris outlined the wheel with light bulbs, a recent invention. The first ride was taken on June 21, 1893, and was a huge success. It cost fifty cents. This was ten times the cost of a ride on a carousel. About 1.5 million people rode the Ferris wheel at the fair.

Check Your Understanding

1. Which word refers to the "greatest number of people allowed"?
   a. doubtful
   b. maximum
   c. cemented
   d. million

2. Which event occurred third?
   a. convincing the committee to accept the Ferris wheel
   b. riding on the Ferris wheel
   c. planning for the Chicago World's Fair
   d. building the Ferris wheel

3. What can you infer about the reasons the committee didn't immediately accept and support the idea of the Ferris wheel?
   a. They didn't think it would work.
   b. They thought it would hold too many people.
   c. They thought it didn't cost enough.
   d. both a and c

4. From the context of the passage, which is the best synonym for **impressive**?
   a. towering
   b. remarkable
   c. ugly
   d. both a and c

/4

Warm-Up **24**

Name ______________________________

Hatshepsut: The Lost Egyptian Queen

Queen Hatshepsut ruled in Egypt from 1479 BCE until 1458 BCE. She was the daughter of **Pharaoh** Thutmose I. He soon recognized her intelligence and curiosity. She was taught to read and write. She was trained to be the wife of a future pharaoh. In her early teens, she was married to her half-brother, Thutmose II. Arranged marriages between brothers and sisters were common for Egyptian kings and queens. It kept power in the family. Thutmose II was sickly. He died a few years after becoming a pharaoh.

Hatshepsut became the person in charge of Egypt while Thutmose III, her husband's son by another wife, was a child. Hatshepsut assumed the powers of a pharaoh. She even wore a false beard as a sign of her power. She sent a trading expedition to the famous kingdom of Punt. This quest returned with many riches. She waged one brief, successful war. She built many monuments, temples, and statues.

When Hatshepsut died, Thutmose III finally became pharaoh. He tried to remove every sign of Hatshepsut's existence. Her name was cut away from stone monuments. Her features were carved off statues. She was unknown until modern historians rediscovered the lost queen of Egypt.

Check Your Understanding

1. From the context of the passage, what is the meaning of **pharaoh**?
   a. a ruler
   b. a person who rules a country in place of a child
   c. a farmer
   d. a person from another country

2. What can you infer about the feelings of Thutmose III from his actions?
   a. He was in love with Hatshepsut.
   b. He was angry at being denied his rightful place as pharaoh for so many years.
   c. He wanted to destroy the people's memory of Hatshepsut.
   d. both b and c

3. From the context of the passage, how can you tell that pharaohs were rarely women?
   a. All of the pharaohs mentioned were men except one.
   b. A beard was a sign of a pharaoh's position.
   c. Women didn't know how to be pharaohs.
   d. both a and b

4. Why did Egyptian rulers sometimes marry one of their sisters?
   a. There were very few girls to choose from.
   b. They wanted to keep power and wealth in the family.
   c. They wanted their sisters to rule.
   d. They wanted to have someone to do the cooking.

/4

Warm-Up 25

Name ______________________________

The Ford Model T

Henry Ford decided to build a family car that working people could afford. His company first built the Model T in 1908. Like other new carmakers, Ford had made cars for the rich, selling as high as $2,800. This was well beyond the money a regular American family could afford to pay for a car. The Model T was different. It was the first car that middle-class families could afford to buy. In 1908, it was priced at $825. However, by 1924, the Model T sold for only $260.

The Model T weighed 1,200 pounds. It carried a ten-gallon gas tank, and it had to be cranked to start the engine. Ford sold fifteen million Model Ts between 1908 and 1927. Ford's great success was based on his use of special methods where each worker placed just one part on each car. The car traveled along a moving belt with just one job for each factory worker. This was very different from the handmade cars built in the early 1900s. Ford also used interchangeable parts. This meant that any engine or wheel, for example, fit on any vehicle.

The prices of Ford's Model T dropped because of his less costly methods of production. He raised his workers' wages. Their lowest wage doubled to $5 a day. The higher pay pushed up pay throughout many industries. This allowed workers in many factories to be able to afford to buy the Model T. Ford changed millions of lives with a single car and a single idea. What ideas do you have? They may be just as valuable!

Check Your Understanding

1. Which of these was a special job in a factory making the Model T?
   a. putting an entire engine together
   b. placing a left rear wheel on an axle
   c. tightening a nut on a wheel
   d. both b and c
2. How many days would a worker have to work to afford the cheapest Model T?
   a. 62
   b. 560
   c. 52
   d. a lifetime
3. Which of these is an accomplishment of Henry Ford?
   a. creating an inexpensive car
   b. cutting wages in the auto industry
   c. raising wages in the auto industry
   d. both a and c
4. Which of these facts would be relevant to the passage?
   a. Many business owners were angry when Ford raised wages.
   b. The Model T came in both car and truck styles.
   c. Women often cranked the Model T to get it started.
   d. all of the above

/4

Warm-Up 26

Name ____________________

The Gibson Homer

The Los Angeles Dodgers began the 1988 World Series as underdogs. Although they had good pitching and solid players, their leader, Kirk Gibson, was hurt. He had injured both legs in the National League playoffs, and he was ill with a stomach virus. Gibson wasn't able to start. When announcer Vin Scully mentioned during the game that Gibson was nowhere to be found on the bench, Kirk sent a note from the locker room to Dodger manager Tommy Lasorda that he was available to pinch-hit. He then went to take some swings in the batting cage.

With a one-run lead in the bottom of the ninth inning, the Oakland Athletics brought in their ace relief pitcher, Dennis Eckersley, to hold the lead. They looked unbeatable. Eckersley got two quick outs, and Dodger fans were almost beyond hope as the game seemed about to be lost. Eckersley walked the next batter, Mike Davis, a respected power hitter, in order to face the light-hitting Dave Anderson who was in the on-deck circle waiting to bat.

Instead of Anderson, Kirk Gibson limped to the plate. He worked the count to three and two. He was barely able to rotate his body or hold the bat after two awkward swings. Following the advice of a coach, he was looking for a slider. It came. Gibson swung and drilled a line drive into the right field seats to win the game. Vin Scully's call said it all: "High fly ball to right field . . . she is . . . gone! In a year that has been so **improbable,** the impossible has happened." An **ecstatic** Gibson pumped his fist and limped home. The Dodgers won the series in five games. Dodger fans who remember this game still cheer with glee.

Check Your Understanding

1. From the context of the passage, what is the best meaning of **ecstatic**?
- a. extremely sad
- b. uncertain
- c. sorrowful
- d. filled with joy

2. Which ball club does the author of the passage appear to favor?
- a. Oakland Athletics
- b. Los Angeles Dodgers
- c. neither club
- d. both clubs

3. From the context of the passage, what is the best meaning of **improbable**?
- a. unlikely to happen
- b. overwhelming odds in favor
- c. best chance to win
- d. impossible

4. Who is Vin Scully?
- a. a baseball announcer
- b. the manager of the Dodgers
- c. the Oakland manager
- d. an Oakland pitcher

/4

Warm-Up 27

Name ____________________

Homer Plessy Refuses to Give Up His Seat

Rosa Parks was not the first African American to refuse to give up her seat on a **segregated** public bus. In fact, the first "bus" was a city streetcar in New Orleans, Louisiana.

The year was 1892. A streetcar was a kind of small train running on rails along the streets of the city. Homer Plessy couldn't find a seat in the "colored" section of the streetcar. He simply moved up to an empty seat in front, even though it was reserved for whites. The conductor of the car immediately had Plessy arrested. He had violated a state law. This law forbade any mixing of the races in most public places. This included streetcars, hotels, and restaurants.

Plessy was as brave as Rosa Parks would be sixty-three years later. He challenged the legality of this state law. This law was the basic tool for enforcing the separation of the races throughout the South. However, the lower courts all ruled against him. They ruled that the state had a right to force these restrictions on African Americans. Homer didn't quit. He took the case all the way through the court system. His final appeal was to the Supreme Court of the United States. This court has the responsibility for deciding if a law is valid under the U.S. Constitution. Plessy lost the decision. A nearly unanimous court ruled against him. The court said that segregation was legal because it offered "separate but equal accommodations." That ruling would finally be overturned in the 1950s by another prominent Supreme Court case, *Brown vs. Board of Education*.

Check Your Understanding

1. Which famous African American is being compared to Homer Plessy in the passage?
   a. Martin Luther King Jr.
   b. Rosa Parks
   c. Jackie Robinson
   d. none of the above

2. From the context of the passage, which of the following is closest in meaning to **segregated**?
   a. separate and apart
   b. illegal
   c. to have different jobs
   d. to live in a special house

3. Which of the following is an example of a unanimous decision?
   a. You and a friend decide to go to the same movie.
   b. Your brother wants lasagna for dinner, but you want salad.
   c. Your mom and dad tell you that you are "grounded."
   d. both a and c

4. From the context of the passage, what can you infer about the personality and character of Homer Plessy?
   a. He didn't give up easily.
   b. He was willing to fight to stop an injustice.
   c. He didn't like riding streetcars.
   d. both a and b

/4

Warm-Up 28

Name ______________________________

Old-Time Country Schools

You might not have enjoyed going to school on the frontier or in rural communities in the years between 1850 and 1880. If you lived on a farm, you might have trudged two to three miles through deep piles of snow to arrive at your one-room wooden schoolhouse. All the grades and age levels were in the same room. The girls sat on one side of the room, and the boys sat on the other. The benches were all the exact same size, with smaller children unable to touch the floor with their feet and larger kids squished on the seats.

You would write your work on a slate and study from one reader until you knew all the lessons. Some rather big boys were often still working on first- or second-grade work. If you didn't know how to spell a word or you misbehaved, the teacher was expected to whack your hand with a heavy ruler. Recess was fifteen minutes in the morning with the girls going out first to play and use the privy, an outhouse that was the bathroom. You ate your lunch near the wood stove in the center of the room. Once it was time to plant crops, many students stayed home to help their families. Your teacher might be a young, unmarried man taking his first job. Part of his income would be staying at a student's home for two weeks at a time. This way, for two weeks, his lodging would be your house for eating and sleeping. Once he had stayed at every home, the school term would be over. Sometimes, your teacher would be a fifteen- or sixteen-year-old girl who taught to earn a little money. Of course, she would have to quit teaching if she got married. Doesn't this school make you appreciate your school today?

Check Your Understanding

1. How were teachers paid in country schools?
   a. They received a little money.
   b. Men often stayed for room and food at student homes.
   c. Teachers made a lot of money.
   d. both a and b
2. What are some contrasts about country schools in the late 1800s and schools today?
   a. Both genders used the same privy.
   b. Students didn't advance until they knew each reader.
   c. Students could have their hand spanked for missing spelling words or bad behavior.
   d. all of the above
3. From the context of the passage, what is the best description of a privy?
   a. a wooden playroom
   b. an outdoor wooden restroom
   c. a place to check your hair
   d. a place to keep pets
4. Who had to quit teaching if they got married?
   a. male teachers
   b. female teachers
   c. both male and female teachers
   d. college teachers

/4

Warm-Up 29

Name ____________________

The Triangle Shirtwaist Factory Fire

On March 25, 1911, a fire broke out in a dress factory in Manhattan, New York. The Triangle Shirtwaist Company, one of many clothing sweatshops in the city, employed more than five hundred workers. Most of them were young immigrant women who were working long hours for very low wages in unsafe and unhealthy conditions. Like most other city workshops, the factory was a firetrap. It had only one fire escape, which was blocked. The emergency doors were locked or blocked from use. Some doors were simply not working. Bosses kept the doors locked to control workers and keep the machines running. The windows on the upper floor were locked. Cloth and other easily burned materials were scattered around everywhere. The machines were old and dangerous.

When the fire started, the terrified workers were trapped by the locked doors. They were also unable to get to the fire escape. Many women on the upper floors were caught in a whirlwind of fire and smoke. They had no choice but to break the windows and jump several floors to the street below. Although police, firemen, and local citizens tried to catch the leaping workers with blankets, most young women who jumped from the upper floors were killed by the fall. Others, afraid to leap, died near the locked doors. Of the more than five hundred employees of the company in the factory that day, 146 were killed. Many others were maimed or burned. The tragedy focused national attention on the problems of sweatshops. Over time, it led to improvements in fire and building **codes**. An excellent children's book about this fire is called *Ashes of Roses* by Mary Jane Auch.

Check Your Understanding

1. From the context of the passage, what is the meaning of **codes**?
   a. a puzzle
   b. a set of rules and regulations
   c. a fire
   d. both a and b
2. Which word refers to "factories with poor working conditions"?
   a. clothes
   b. sweatshops
   c. immigrants
   d. maimed
3. What kind of garments were made in the Triangle Shirtwaist Factory?
   a. dress shirts
   b. slacks
   c. dresses
   d. hats
4. Which fact would be informative if added to the passage?
   a. Other garment factories also had fires.
   b. Many immigrant women were taken advantage of in sweatshops.
   c. Union leaders tried to get better working conditions.
   d. all of the above

/4

Warm-Up 30

Name ____________________

Making Maple Syrup

Farm children of the past who lived in New England and neighboring states often helped make maple syrup. Maple trees were very common, and the winters were cold. Trees in these cold areas freeze during the winter, and the flow of water from the ground to the top of the trees simply freezes in place. In the spring, the ground thaws and the weather is warmer. Then the **sap** in the trees starts flowing again in the millions of little tubes within the wood of the trees.

In the past, children, or their fathers, drilled two or three narrow holes into the wood of each tree. They placed a thin tube, often a hollow piece of wood or metal, into each hole. They hung a wooden or metal pail from each tube sticking out from the tree, or they set the pails on the ground beneath each tube. The sap, which was now liquid, would rise up the tubes in the tree again. It would drip out of the hollow tube into the pail. Children collected the pails of very cold, sweet sap. They poured the sap into black metal **cauldrons** that were hanging over a blazing hot wood fire.

The water was partly boiled away from the sap, and a sweet maple syrup was left. Some of the syrup was cooled into cakes of hard, brown maple sugar. Today, maple sugar is much more expensive and less common than cane sugar. Modern collection systems from **groves** of maple trees use more machines. However, some people still make maple syrup the old-fashioned way for the sake of tradition.

Check Your Understanding

1. From the context of the passage, what is the most informative description of **sap**?
   a. water in tree leaves
   b. maple syrup
   c. water in a tree
   d. water flowing up the tubes of a tree and flavored by the sugar in the wood

2. From the context of the passage, what is the best description of a **cauldron**?
   a. a pot
   b. a teapot
   c. a black kettle for boiling
   d. a bucket

3. From the context of the passage, what is the best meaning of **groves**?
   a. small groups of trees
   b. forests
   c. tall maple trees
   d. trees grown from seeds

4. Which of the following sentences would be the best one to add to the last paragraph?
   a. The sap is only good for syrup in the spring.
   b. The tiny wooden tubes in trees are called *xylem*.
   c. Maple syrup is very expensive in markets today.
   d. American Indians taught early settlers how to make maple syrup.

/4

Did You Know?

Warm-Up

Name ______________________________

1 Your Meniscus Is Leaking

You may have done this at the kitchen table when no one was looking. You filled a glass up to the brim with water to see how far you could fill it before it spilled. Then you kept pouring the water, and it didn't spill—at least not right away.

Don't try this at the table. Take it outside where the spilled water can just evaporate. Fill a glass with water until it is exactly even with the lip of the container. Then slowly and carefully pour a tiny stream of water into the full glass. Keep your eyes level with the lip of the glass. Do you see a kind of bubble above the lip? This bubble of water is called a **meniscus**. It is formed because molecules of water have a strong attraction to each other. This is the same kind of attraction that magnets have.

The bubble you see happens because of something called surface tension. This is what allows some insects to walk on water. It also helps you to float on water or swim. You can feel the surface tension when you draw your hand through water. The resistance of the water is created by the attraction of water molecules. A single drop of water has 1,700,000,000,000,000,000,000,000 (1.7 septillion) molecules. And every molecule is attracted to every other molecule. The next time someone pours a glass of water and it begins to spill over, tell the person his or her meniscus is leaking. Don't forget to explain what you mean!

Check Your Understanding

1. From the context of the passage, which word is the best synonym for **meniscus**?
   a. molecule
   b. attraction
   c. bubble
   d. tension
2. Which natural force allows the meniscus to form?
   a. the attraction of water molecules to each other
   b. the evaporation of water
   c. water bugs walking on water
   d. gravity
3. Which of the following would be a good title for the passage?
   a. "Why Water Is Wet"
   b. "Walking on Water"
   c. "How a Meniscus Is Formed"
   d. "Why Water Spills"
4. What would happen if water molecules weren't attracted to each other?
   a. People would be able to float easier.
   b. No meniscus would form on a glass of water.
   c. Many water insects would be unable to walk on water.
   d. both b and c

/4

Warm-Up 2

Name ____________________

The Compass in Your Nose

You have a compass in your nose. It is a very small trace of iron located in the ethmoid bone between your eyes. This tiny piece of iron helps humans in direction finding. The iron is attracted to Earth's magnetic force, just as a compass pointer is attracted toward Earth's magnetic North Pole.

The human magnet works better on some people than on others. People have been tested on their ability to use this power. They have been blindfolded so they cannot see clues, such as the sun or the direction of objects. They are still often able to face north just as a compass needle does. However, some people are much better at this than others.

Tests have been done with magnets to prove this effect. Magnets placed near the right side of the head caused people to move to the right. Magnets placed to the left caused people to want to move to the left. This experiment proves that humans seem to be affected by magnetic fields. Many other animals, such as pigeons, salmon, dolphins, and honeybees, have the same ability to react to magnetic force. Try the experiment yourself and see if your personal "nose compass" is working!

Check Your Understanding

1. Where is the human compass located?
   a. in the nostrils
   b. in the brain
   c. in the bone between the eyes
   d. in the tip of the nose
2. In which direction does the compass help orient humans?
   a. west
   b. north
   c. south
   d. east
3. What might cause the compass in your nose to be disoriented in the wrong direction?
   a. bright sunlight
   b. standing near machinery with a strong magnet or electromagnet
   c. wind
   d. the moon
4. Which of the following can you infer from the passage?
   a. Humans are always aware that they are affected by magnetic fields.
   b. People should carry a magnet with them.
   c. Some people are more sensitive to magnetic fields than others.
   d. both a and c

/4

Warm-Up

3

Name ______________________________

Snail Training

Garden snails are gastropods, which means "stomach-footed." Most types of snails live in water, but these land creatures still need water. When the weather is hot and dry, they climb up a wall or branch and **estivate**, a process similar to hibernation. They seal their shells with thick mucus and don't move until rain falls or a damp evening arrives. Wet weather provides a pleasant opportunity to find soft, wet plant food.

Because of their fondness for wet environments, snails can be trained to do several tricks. Place one or two garden snails on a wet paper towel and dampen the snails with water. They will soon emerge from their shells and glide along the paper towel eating some of it. You can soak a piece of yarn or thick string and gently place the snail on the yarn. If you hold both ends of the wet yarn tightly, the snail will slowly glide along the yarn from one side to the other. It will also climb up the yarn if you hold it vertically, although even snails can lose their grip and fall off. Snails will even paint a picture, if you put them in wet food coloring and give them a piece of shiny paper to decorate. And who wouldn't want a piece of art by a gastropod? It's truly one of a kind!

Check Your Understanding

1. What was the author's intent in writing the passage?
   a. to describe the behavior of snails
   b. to provide interesting ways to study the snail's movement
   c. to help the reader learn to eat snails
   d. both a and b
2. From the context of the passage, which word has a similar meaning to **estivate**?
   a. late
   b. gastropod
   c. hibernate
   d. move
3. What encourages snails to come out of their shells?
   a. wind
   b. grass
   c. moisture
   d. sunlight
4. Why are snails called gastropods?
   a. They move on their stomachs.
   b. They have pods on their bellies.
   c. They hide their feet in their stomachs.
   d. They need shoes to walk.

/4

Warm-Up 4

Name ____________________

Earthworm Pets

Earthworms make fascinating pets. House your worms in a small box or plastic container. Be sure to collect several earthworms because they thrive better in groups than alone or in pairs. Perhaps they get lonely. Fill the box with soft soil and plant materials, such as leaves, grass, or vegetables. Try different plants to determine their favorite foods. Worms **decompose** plant matter and pass the digested matter out as "casts," which enrich soil and make it excellent for plant growth. Earthworms need to be damp to breathe oxygen through their skins, but they will be forced out of water-filled tunnels because they cannot breathe in them. Earthworm tunnels loosen the soil, allowing water to penetrate and plants to sprout.

Observe how worms pull themselves along by stretching and contracting their long, segmented bodies. Use a magnifying glass to find the four pairs of tiny bristles on each segment. They use these bristles to help grip the walls of the tunnel or the soil above ground. Shine a flashlight on worms moving in the dark and notice their reactions. They "see" with their skin, which is light sensitive. Worms also react to some sounds but ignore others, so try playing different notes to your pet worms using a musical instrument to see which they like. Gently pet the worms and observe their reactions. Don't be squeamish; instead, enjoy these unusual pets!

Check Your Understanding

1. How does the author feel about worms?
   a. disgusted
   b. interested and enthusiastic
   c. bored
   d. angry
2. What does light-sensitive skin do?
   a. It helps worms react to light.
   b. It blinds them.
   c. It improves their eyesight.
   d. It covers their skin with eyes.
3. Which senses does the author suggest you test on your worms?
   a. touch
   b. sound
   c. skin sensitivity to light
   d. all of the above
4. From the content of the passage, what is the meaning of **decompose**?
   a. to decay or break down
   b. to die
   c. to hold or grasp
   d. to give birth

/4

Warm-Up

Name ______________________________

5 The Invention of Silly Putty®

Some of the best inventions happened purely by accident. James Wright was an engineer working for General Electric. While working in his lab one day, he accidentally mixed boric acid and silicone oil in a test tube. The substance he created was called a polymer. This is a substance consisting of giant molecules formed by chaining together many simpler molecules. This polymer had very different properties. It could bounce higher than a rubber ball. It could be stretched for a long distance without tearing. It did not rot or decay. It could even copy an image, like old newspaper print and comics, if pressed flat against the substance.

No one knew what to do with this new invention until a toy merchant came up with an idea. He realized that the material would make a great toy for children and adults. In 1949, it hit the market packaged in twelve little plastic eggs and sold to families as "nutty putty." Later, the name was changed to Silly Putty®. It became one of the most popular toys of all time. Silly Putty is sold all over the world. It has never lost its popularity. More than nine million pounds of this strange substance have been sold. That's quite a record for an accidental invention!

Check Your Understanding

1. Which two chemicals were mixed to create Silly Putty?
   a. boric acid and oxygen
   b. vinegar and silicone oil
   c. silicone oil and boric acid
   d. acids and bases

2. What word describes "a substance with different properties and giant molecules made by chaining together smaller molecules"?
   a. silicone
   b. boric acid
   c. molecules
   d. polymer

3. What can you infer about the copying ability of Silly Putty?
   a. It appealed only to scientists.
   b. Parents and children enjoyed the product because it could be used in so many ways.
   c. It was only successful in the United States.
   d. It doesn't copy modern newspapers and comics as well as it did older ones.

4. What is the main idea of the passage?
   a. Silly Putty is a successful accidental invention.
   b. Silly Putty is still very popular.
   c. Silly Putty is a polymer.
   d. Silly Putty was a great invention.

/4

Warm-Up 6

Name ______________________________

Your Hair Is Dead

The hair on your head, arms, and any other place on your body is dead protein pushed through the skin by hair follicles. There are about five million hair follicles throughout the human body. You have approximately 120,000 follicles on your head. You have about 108,000 hairs on your head at any one time. If your hair averages two inches in length, you have 18,000 feet of hair on your head. If the hair on your head averages five inches long, you have about 45,000 feet of hair on your head. The average hair on your head grows about half an inch a month, and it grows fastest in the morning. You lose about seventy hairs a day. Your body will produce about one hundred feet of dead protein in a day and seven miles of hair in a year.

Hair **hibernates**. It grows in cycles. On the scalp, each hair grows continuously for three to five years and then enters a resting phase of about three months or so. The hair is shed but not replaced immediately. After another resting phase of several months, the follicle produces a new hair. You don't have to worry too much though. About 90 percent of the scalp is in the growing phase at all times. Eyebrow hairs stay short because their growing phase only lasts ten weeks. Eyelashes are replaced about every three months. You will grow about six hundred complete eyelashes in a lifetime. So brush your hair and enjoy it!

Check Your Understanding

1. What is the meaning of the term **hibernates**, when referring to hair?
   a. Hair goes through several colors.
   b. Hair sleeps every night.
   c. Hair grows in cycles and then enters a resting phase.
   d. Hair falls out and leaves you bald.

2. How often are eyelashes replaced?
   a. every ten weeks
   b. every three to five years
   c. every six months
   d. every three months

3. What is the author's purpose in writing the passage?
   a. to encourage you to care for your hair
   b. to entertain the reader
   c. to inform the reader
   d. to change your mind

4. What can you infer about your own hair from the passage?
   a. Some of the hair follicles are in a resting phase right now.
   b. Hair grows at different rates in different parts of the body.
   c. Red hair grows faster than black hair.
   d. both a and b

/4

Warm-Up 7

Name ____________________

How Big Is a Googol?

Mathematician Edward Kasner wrote the number 1 followed by 100 zeroes: 10,000,00 0,000,000,000,000,000,000,000,000,000,000, 000,000,000,000,000,000,000,000,000,000,00 0,000,000,000,000,000,000,000,000,000,000. He asked his nine-year-old nephew, Milton, to suggest a name for such a huge number. Milton immediately suggested "Googol." The name stuck.

Because 100 is 10 times 10, and 1,000 is 10 times 100, Googol truly is a gigantic number. If you added all of the hairs on your head and all the hairs on the heads of all the people alive, you wouldn't equal a googol. If you included the hairs of all of the animals on Earth, you still wouldn't equal a googol. The number is so large that it is believed to be much more than the total of all of the atoms in the universe.

There is a short way to write a googol. You can write it as an **exponent**: 10^{100}, which is said "10 to the hundredth power." It's shorter, but it is still just as powerful a number. If you want to express an even more gigantic number, you can write a googolplex, which is a googol to the googol power written as 10^{googol}. It might be hard for you to find a use for such an enormous number, but you can try!

Check Your Understanding

1. What is the best and most complete definition of an **exponent**?
- a. a power
- b. a number multiplied by 10
- c. a number multiplied by itself
- d. a math expression specifying how many times a number is multiplied by itself

2. From the context of the passage, which of the following statements can you infer to be true?
- a. A googol is smaller than the number of animals in the world.
- b. A googol is smaller than the number of plants in the world.
- c. A googol is smaller than the number of people in the world.
- d. A googol is larger than the number of grains of sand on all of the beaches of the world.

3. Which of the following statements is true about a googolplex?
- a. A googol is larger than a googolplex.
- b. It would take you a year to count to a googolplex.
- c. A googolplex is a googol to the googol power.
- d. A googolplex has a value of about one million.

4. Who invented the name "googol"?
- a. a computer
- b. Edward Kasner
- c. Kasner's nephew, Milton
- d. Dr. Googol

/4

Warm-Up 8

Name ______________________________

Sharks Are Survivors

A few swimmers are attacked and about six people are killed every year by sharks. Humans kill about one hundred million sharks every year. They are used for animal food, necklaces, fertilizer, shark-fin soup, shoes, wallets, and many other products. Sharks have been in existence for at least three hundred million years. They existed before, during, and after the dinosaur era. Today, there are about five hundred species of sharks living in the world's oceans. These seaborne predators are just as important to the ecology of the oceans as wolves, lions, bears, and other land predators are to the balance of nature on land.

The smallest shark in the world is the dwarf lantern shark. It is about the size of a chocolate bar and feeds on small shrimp. The great white shark grows to at least twenty-three feet long. It is the largest **predatory** shark. For skin, all sharks have tiny tooth-like scales as tough as sandpaper. They have gill slits for breathing oxygen from water and jaws that can shoot forward to grab prey. Each jaw has rows of razor-sharp replaceable teeth. Some sharks use 20,000 teeth in a lifetime. A shark's skin is as sensitive as fingertips are to humans. Their ears can detect sounds too low for humans to hear. Their nostrils can detect scents in water. Gel pits in the nose can detect electrical impulses from the nerves of other animals. Sharks were designed for survival.

Check Your Understanding

1. What is the main idea of the passage?
- a. Sharks eat too many people.
- b. Sharks have sensitive nostrils.
- c. Sharks are designed for survival and have survived a long time.
- d. Sharks are useful to man.

2. From the context of the passage, what is the meaning of **predatory**?
- a. lives on plants
- b. hunts and eats prey
- c. man-eating
- d. friendly

3. Which of the following is a survival feature of sharks?
- a. the ability to detect electrical impulses in water
- b. the ability to detect smells in water
- c. the ability to hear low sounds
- d. all of the above

4. Which word in the passage refers to the relationship between living things and their environment?
- a. seaborne
- b. predatory
- c. ecology
- d. survival

/4

Warm-Up 9

Name ______________________________

LEGO® Bricks

LEGO® bricks were invented by an out-of-work carpenter in Denmark. He started a small toy-making business in 1932. The carpenter named the business "LEGO" after two Danish words, "play well." After starting his business, it took him over fifteen years to invent LEGO bricks. They were based on his wooden block carvings. The blocks interlocked and allowed a child to build with them. They were made of plastic and called Automatic Binding Bricks at first. The blocks had studs on top and were hollow underneath. They could easily be stacked and locked with each other. The first two colors were red and white. They were soon followed by green, blue, and yellow. The **unique** toy was an instant hit in Denmark and other European countries. It reached the United States in 1961 and was very popular by the 1970s. A special feature of LEGO toys is that the bricks can be arranged in more than a million different ways.

LEGO bricks can be made in about ten seconds from a kind of plastic. It is heated like bread dough. The material is pressed into molds and cooled. Out of every one million LEGO bricks made, only about twenty-six are rejected. Today, the LEGO Group sells more than 1,700 different shapes of LEGO bricks in every possible color. In the fifty years after its invention, more than 203 million LEGO building bricks have been made. This is why the LEGO Group is the fifth largest maker of toys. When is the last time you built something with LEGO bricks?

Check Your Understanding

1. Which of the following is a reasonable conclusion based on the passage?
   a. LEGO bricks have remained popular for over fifty years.
   b. Wooden building blocks lock together as easily as LEGO bricks.
   c. All children love using LEGO bricks.
   d. both a and b
2. From the context of the passage, what is the best meaning of **unique**?
   a. one
   b. special and different
   c. made of plastic
   d. appealing to children
3. Which of the following is the best topic sentence in the passage?
   a. paragraph one, second sentence
   b. paragraph one, sixth sentence
   c. paragraph two, second sentence
   d. paragraph two, sixth sentence
4. Which of the following information would be irrelevant to the passage?
   a. There are LEGOLAND parks in three nations.
   b. The LEGO Company was created in 1932 before LEGO bricks were invented.
   c. Tinkertoys® are sometimes used by children to build things.
   d. Ole Kirk Kristiansen invented LEGO bricks in Denmark.

/4

Warm-Up 10

Name ______________________________

QWERTY

The first practical typewriter was created in 1867 by Christopher Sholes and Carlos Glidden. The two inventors also designed the standard keyboard layout. It is nicknamed QWERTY for the first six letters on the top line of the keyboard. The arrangement seems senseless. However, it was designed to prevent the keys on mechanical typewriters from catching each other. If they got caught, the typist had to stop typing and pull them apart.

The QWERTY arrangement forced typists to work a little slower. Some letters were placed in hard to reach places. For example, *A* is beneath the little finger on the left hand. *A* is a commonly used letter, but it is assigned to the weakest finger. Therefore, it takes a bit more time to type. *E* is the most used letter in the English language, but *E* is placed on the top row. It is harder to reach. The middle row has the easiest-to-reach letters, but they are not the most commonly used. Some letter combinations like *sh* and *th* were placed apart from each other. As a result, typewriting keys were less likely to get caught with each other.

Why don't we invent a new and simplified keyboard arrangement? Millions of people would be required to learn a new system. The manual typewriter may be long gone, but quirky QWERTY is alive and likely to remain in use for decades to come.

Check Your Understanding

1. From the context of the passage, what is the meaning of the word "QWERTY"?
   a. manual typewriter
   b. questions asked
   c. quick eraser
   d. It has no meaning.
2. What conclusion can you draw from reading the passage?
   a. People should type with only two fingers.
   b. Everybody wants a new keyboard design.
   c. Everybody should return to using manual typewriters.
   d. The keyboard system was designed for a useful purpose.
3. What inference can you draw from the last paragraph?
   a. People would probably resist changes to the standard keyboard design.
   b. Nobody should use typewriters.
   c. QWERTY is a new computer design.
   d. Everybody should use computers.
4. Why is the letter *E* on the top row of the keyboard?
   a. It is easier to reach there.
   b. It is the most used letter in English.
   c. It is a little harder to reach in that location.
   d. Nobody ever uses the letter.

/4

Warm-Up **11**

Name ______________________________

Grizzly Bears

Grizzly bears are usually dark brown, but they vary from yellow-brown to black. White-tipped hairs provide the "grizzled" appearance that gives them their name. Grizzlies have a distinctive hump of solid muscle over the shoulders that gives them great strength. They can weigh from 320 to 1,500 pounds. The Alaskan Brown Bear, a grizzly, can reach 1,700 pounds, making it the largest land carnivore.

Although they usually avoid humans, grizzlies are immensely strong, unpredictable, and dangerous. They can bite through iron, bend rifle barrels, slice open cars with their claws, and smash through cabin doors looking for food. Running as fast as thirty-five miles an hour, they can easily outrun a person. Grizzlies are **omnivorous** feeders. They kill and eat large mammals, such as elk, moose, mountain goats, sheep, and cattle. They eat carrion, or dead animals, killed by other predators. They also eat fish, especially salmon, which they catch during spawning season. Grizzlies are nimble enough to catch mice, squirrels, and other small mammals and insects. They feed on many kinds of plants, including roots, sprouts, berries, and fungi.

During its winter sleep, a grizzly will lose about two pounds a day and may wake up from its sleep at half its weight. They are not true hibernators and are easily awakened. Grizzlies give birth in their dens during the winter. They care for their cubs for as long as five years. A grizzly's life span in the wild ranges from fifteen to thirty-four years.

Check Your Understanding

1. From the context of the passage, what is the meaning of **omnivorous**?
   a. picky eater
   b. eats only meat
   c. eats only plants
   d. eats both plant and animal foods

2. What color is suggested by the word "grizzled" to describe the bears' appearance?
   a. white or streaked with white
   b. jet black
   c. dark brown or streaked with dark brown
   d. yellow or streaked with yellow

3. What should people avoid doing when they are in an area frequented by bears?
   a. screaming and chasing after a bear
   b. running away from a bear
   c. leaving food out in cars and cabins
   d. all of the above

4. Which word refers to "the decaying flesh of a dead animal"?
   a. omnivorous
   b. carrion
   c. hibernators
   d. grizzled

/4

Warm-Up **12** Name ______________________

Slinkity Slinkys®

The Slinky® was invented by Richard James, a naval engineer during World War II. He was experimenting with coiled tension springs. He was trying to design a meter to measure horsepower for ships. James dropped one of the coiled springs on the floor one day and was both amazed and amused to watch the spring "walk" across the floor. He played and experimented with the spring to see what else he could make it do.

James immediately recognized the appeal the spring would have as a toy. He experimented with many versions, trying to determine which length of wire and which thickness would be best. He eventually settled on eighty feet of thin, coiled wire. His wife, Betty, is given credit for the name Slinky, which is derived from a Swedish word meaning **sinuous**. The name also sounds a little like the "slinkity" noise that the toy makes when it "walks."

The first versions of the toy were sold in Gimbels Department Store in Philadelphia in 1945 for $1.00. It was an instant hit, selling four hundred in less than two hours. Slinkys are now sold on six continents. Enough wire has been used in making Slinkys to circle the world more than 130 times. The distance around the world at the equator is about 25,000 miles. That is a lot of wire for a lot of Slinkys!

Check Your Understanding

1. From the context of the passage, what is the meaning of **sinuous**?
  a. unusual
  b. bending or winding in and out
  c. evil
  d. short and thin

2. Which of the following is a good summary of the article?
  a. Slinkys are fun to play with.
  b. The Slinky is a successful toy resulting from an accidental discovery and careful experimentation.
  c. The Slinky was first used to measure speed in naval ships.
  d. Slinkys are made from coiled wire.

3. What can you infer from the information in the last paragraph?
  a. Slinkys are still a popular toy.
  b. Slinkys are no longer sold in the United States.
  c. There is no longer enough wire to make Slinkys.
  d. The only place you can buy Slinkys is in Philadelphia at Gimbels.

4. On which of the seven continents are Slinkys probably *not* sold?
  a. North America
  b. Europe
  c. Asia
  d. Antarctica

/4

Warm-Up **13**

Name ______________________________

Keeping Toads and Frogs

Toads and frogs are well-known amphibians. They live on land and in water. Toads are squat and plump and have rough, warty-looking skin and webbed, rear feet. North American frogs are large with slim waists, long legs, pointed toes, and webbed, hind feet. Frogs and toads can be kept in a small plastic or glass aquarium. Divide the aquarium into a water area and a muddy section by using small pebbles or a piece of plastic. It's important that frogs and toads keep their skin damp at all times.

Both toads and frogs eat insects, which you can collect outside or purchase from any pet store. Live mealworm larvae, crickets, flies, and other similar prey will satisfy them immensely. Watch a toad as it eagerly prepares to catch its prey. The toad's eyes spot movement, and it watches the prey carefully and gauges the distance between itself and its intended target. Sometimes, the toad will creep a little closer or just raise its body. The tongue of the common toad is attached to the front of its mouth and is sticky, but it flicks out like a whip to catch its prey. Then it easily snatches the prey back into its mouth. The toad may also use its front foot to push large insects into its mouth. It closes its eyes as it swallows the food. Toads can sometimes be trained to eat dead prey if the insect is dangled in front of the toad on a string. See for yourself which other foods toads or frogs will eat! Enjoy watching your toads and frogs before returning them to their natural environment.

Check Your Understanding

1. What word refers to animals that live on both land and water?
   a. prey
   b. warty
   c. amphibian
   d. gauges

2. In which sentences would you find information to compare and contrast frogs and toads?
   a. paragraph two, sentences one through four
   b. paragraph two, sentences five through eight
   c. paragraph one, sentences one through four
   d. paragraph one, sentences five through eight

3. What part of a toad's body is compared to a whip?
   a. front leg
   b. tongue
   c. eye
   d. rear leg

4. Why do you think the passage says you should return your frog or toad to its natural environment?
   a. to preserve the balance of nature
   b. to respect all living creatures
   c. to recognize the importance of all creatures in the wild
   d. all of the above

/4

Warm-Up 14

Name ______________________________

Save That Pencil

Students tend to lose their pencils, break them without thinking, and find all sorts of non-writing uses for them. The pencil in your hand is one of the most remarkable and useful tools in the world. A man named Friedrich Staedtler invented the modern "lead" pencil in about 1622 in Germany. He was the first person to mass-produce them.

Staedtler did not use lead, and there is no lead in your pencil. However, some pencils did use lead until the early twentieth century. Lead will make a mark, but it is **toxic** and not safe to use either in the hands or around the face and mouth where many pencils sometimes stray. Staedtler used black graphite, a soft form of carbon.

Graphite is still used today. It is mixed with clay and wax and heated to high temperatures. The modern pencil is a superb piece of technology. The pencil is less messy than ink, can be easily erased, and makes clear, dark, smooth, and smudge-free lines. The modern pencil can produce a continuous line twenty-two miles long. That's a distance of 116,160 foot-long rulers laid end to end. Enjoy your pencil. For a few cents each, it is a remarkable bargain.

Check Your Understanding

1. Which is *not* a reason pencils are useful?
   a. Their mark can be easily erased.
   b. They make smooth lines.
   c. They are not messy.
   d. They don't break.

2. From the context of the passage, what is the meaning of **toxic**?
   a. pretty
   b. delicious
   c. poisonous
   d. clean

3. Which of these statements can you infer from the passage?
   a. Every pencil is used for twenty-two miles of writing.
   b. Finding a useful, inexpensive writing material was important to people in earlier times.
   c. Students put pencils in or near their mouths.
   d. both b and c

4. Which of these sentences is a topic sentence in paragraph three?
   a. The modern pencil is a superb piece of technology.
   b. Staedtler used black graphite, a soft form of carbon.
   c. Staedtler invented the modern "lead" pencil about 1622 in Germany.
   d. For a few cents each, it is a remarkable bargain.

/4

Warm-Up 15

Name ______________________________

The Safety Pin

The safety pin was designed to hold separate pieces of cloth together. It was invented on April 10, 1849, because the inventor owed a friend $15. Walter Hunt was a mechanic who lived in New York. He felt obliged to repay his debt right away. Hunt experimented with a piece of wire for three hours that afternoon. He designed the safety pin with a spring and a clasp to hold the pin in place. Hunt created the model and wrote the design and application for the patent. He sold the invention that day for $400. He immediately paid back his $15 debt.

Hunt never received another penny for this invention. Stores have sold millions of dollars worth of safety pins, and the pin is still in use today. During the course of his lifetime, Hunt also designed and created a streetcar bell and a stove that burned hard coal. He created a flax-spinning machine and a knife sharpener. Hunt built a repeating rifle and a nail-making machine. Hunt made a paper collar for dress shirts of the day. This inventive genius also designed an ice plow, a metal bullet that exploded, and an early version of the sewing machine. He never patented the sewing machine because he didn't want to put seamstresses out of work. His new machine would have cost them their jobs. For all of his creative gadgets and clever ideas, Walter Hunt never seemed to make much money. However, he made life easier for a lot of people.

Check Your Understanding

1. From the context of the passage, what conclusion can you draw about the character and personality of Walter Hunt?
   a. Hunt was creative and imaginative.
   b. Walter was persistent in working on a project.
   c. Hunt felt obligated to pay off his debts promptly.
   d. all of the above

2. What is a clasp used for on a safety pin?
   a. a metal fastener to hold things together
   b. a hand grip
   c. a spring
   d. a circle

3. Which piece of information would be least relevant to the passage?
   a. Hunt recognized simple needs that people had for daily life.
   b. Hunt belonged to a religious group who believed in being self-sufficient, reliable, and trustworthy.
   c. He patented his invention.
   d. the name of the person to whom Hunt owed money

4. Which of the following is an opinion and *not* a fact?
   a. Walter Hunt was the greatest inventor of all time.
   b. Everyone should be an inventor.
   c. Walter Hunt created several inventions.
   d. both a and b

/4

Warm-Up 16

Name ______________________________

Count to One Billion

Suppose you were offered one billion dollars. However, first you had to count every dollar using these rules:

1. You must count one dollar every second.
2. You must count for eight hours every day with no breaks.
3. You must count every day of the year.
4. You must take off one day each leap year.
5. You must count every year until you reach one billion.

How long do you think it would take until you counted one billion dollars?

You can count $60 in one minute and $3,600 in one hour. You can count $28,800 in one eight-hour day. You can count $10,512,000 in one year. In 10 years, you could count $105,120,000. In 90 years, you could count $946,080,000. In 95 years, you could count $998,640,000. You would have to spend 95 years, 47 days, 1 hour, 46 minutes, and 40 seconds to count one billion dollars. You might be sick of money and too tired to care by that time!

Check Your Understanding

1. How long would it take to count one billion dollars?

a. more than 95 years
b. less than 47 years
c. about 15 years
d. about 30 years

2. According to the passage, how many days in the year would you count?

a. 60 days
b. 300 days
c. 365 days
d. 7 days

3. Using your knowledge of math, about how long would it take to count one billion dollars in $10 dollar bills instead of $1 dollar bills?

a. about 95 years
b. about 30 years
c. about 9 ½ years
d. about 60 years

4. Using your knowledge of math, about how long would it take to count one billion dollars in $100 dollar bills instead of $1 dollar bills?

a. about 10 years
b. about 2 years
c. about 4 years
d. less than 1 year

/4

Warm-Up 17

Name ____________________

Tsunamis

Tsunamis are extremely high waves. They occur when the sea floor is shaken by a major earthquake or volcano. These waves have nothing to do with tides and are not tidal waves. The name *tsunami* is a Japanese word for "harbor wave." Waves of a tsunami may travel almost unnoticed in deep water away from an earthquake or volcanic eruption. They travel along the seabed as fast as a jet plane. They can travel over four hundred miles an hour. As they near shallow coastal waters, the water rears up into waves of one hundred feet or higher. These waves smash into harbors and coasts. They destroy boats and buildings as if they were toys. They drown most living things in their paths. The water may come in a series of a dozen or more waves. They can hit every few minutes.

Local quakes may generate a tsunami in as few as fifteen minutes. But if a quake occurred near Japan, the tsunami may hit across the Pacific Ocean hours later. The highest tsunami wave ever recorded was over 1,700 feet high. It struck the Alaskan coast in 1958. A powerful tsunami in 2004 hit coasts in Asia, killing more than 200,000 people. Be aware of tsunamis and know what to do in case one is forecast near you.

Check Your Understanding

1. Which of these titles would be best for the passage?
   a. "Tidal Waves Hit Japan"
   b. "Tsunamis Cause Some Damage"
   c. "How Tsunamis Occur and What They Do"
   d. "Japan and Tsunamis"

2. Which of the following events cause tsunamis to occur?
   a. earthquakes
   b. tidal waves
   c. volcanoes
   d. both a and c

3. Where do tsunamis cause most of their damage?
   a. far out in the ocean
   b. near harbors and coasts
   c. near deserted beaches
   d. both a and c

4. From the context of the passage, what can you infer that you should do when news of a tsunami is forecast?
   a. Go to the beach and watch it hit.
   b. Get as far inland away from harbors and coasts as possible.
   c. Watch the tsunami from your hotel room.
   d. Get into a boat and sail away.

/4

Warm-Up 18

Name ______________________________

Skunks

Skunks have a rather bad reputation among humans. They are usually **solitary** creatures, although they do share dens with other skunks. This happens frequently during the winter when they sleep during freezing cold weather. Their dens are located among rocks, in storm drains, in burrows between rocks, and in woodpiles. You can often see skunks at night going about their business of finding food, such as insects, grubs, small mammals, fruit, and bird and turtle eggs, along with kitchen garbage.

Skunks have few natural enemies except the great horned owl, a night predator with a very poor sense of smell. The skunk's spray consists of seven different chemicals and is so strong that it can cause temporary blindness in people and pets. However, most skunks give fair warning before they spray. Some skunks stamp their feet. The spotted skunk does a handstand and walks with its rear feet in the air before firing its spray. The sticky spray is squirted from glands under the skunk's tail. It can hit a target twenty feet away but is only accurate up to about seven feet. However, the smell can be detected a mile away. Skunks carry enough spray for five or six loads. The striped skunk can fire off its spray even when held in the air by its tail. Skunks are a major carrier of rabies, and bites to people or pets are dangerous. Skunks are seldom afraid of humans and are sometimes sold as pets—after a descenting operation, of course.

Check Your Understanding

1. How accurate is the skunk's spray?
   a. up to twenty feet
   b. one mile
   c. about five feet
   d. up to seven feet

2. What are the main predators of skunks?
   a. humans
   b. small mammals
   c. foxes
   d. great horned owls

3. From the context of the passage, which is an antonym for **solitary**?
   a. social
   b. lonely
   c. meat-eating
   d. scented

4. What dangers does skunk spray pose to people and animals?
   a. temporary blindness
   b. death
   c. rabies
   d. both a and c

/4

Warm-Up 19

Name ____________________

The Latin in Your English

Latin, the common language of the Ancient Romans, is one root of English. We use many Latin expressions in English, especially in law and in common sayings. If something is done *sub rosa*, it is done in secret. You can graduate from high school or college *summa cum laude*, meaning "with the highest praise." This may happen at your school, which is your *alma mater*, or nurturing mother. The school acts *in* ***loco*** *parentis*, meaning "in the place of your parents." You may have had an *annus mirabilis*, or a wonderful, remarkable, miraculous year. Your other self is your *alter ego*. You hope to live with *mens sana in corpore sano* (a sound mind in a sound body).

A person unwanted in a country or any community is *persona non grata*. On the other hand, a respected leader may be *primus inter pares*—first among equals who works *pro patria*, or for his or her country. This person would surely not be *non compos mentis*, which translates to "not of sound mind, or insane." A person caught in the very act of committing a crime is *flagrante delicto*, but he or she will be tried *ex post facto* (after the deed). The murder victim or evidence in a crime is called the *corpus delicti*. A judge often considers *cui bono*, or who stands to benefit from a crime.

How many of these Latin expressions did you know before reading this?

Check Your Understanding

1. From the context of the passage, what Latin word means "sound or healthy"?
   a. *sano*
   b. *mens*
   c. *sana*
   d. both a and c

2. From the context of the passage, what is the meaning of **loco** in the Latin phrase *in loco parentis*?
   a. place
   b. person
   c. body
   d. country

3. From the context of the passage, what can you infer is the meaning of the Latin term *patria*?
   a. father
   b. country
   c. person
   d. crazy

4. From the context in the passage, which of the following Latin phrases means "love of country"?
   a. *amor patriae*
   b. *ipso facto*
   c. *ne plus ultra*
   d. all of the above

/4

Warm-Up 20

Name ______________________________

Heartbeats

Clench your fist. Place it on your chest a little left of center. Your heart is about the size of your fist and is located about two-thirds down on the left side of your chest. It expands and contracts about 70 times a minute in a healthy adult man. Each expansion and contraction is one heartbeat. An average adult woman's heart beats about 78 times a minute. It beats about 85 to 90 times a minute for a sixth-grader and 130 times a minute in a baby.

The heart pumps blood around the body through 16,000 miles of arteries, veins, and capillaries in the circulatory system. Blood is pumped to the lungs to carry oxygen to other parts of the body and from other parts of the body back to the heart to receive more oxygen. Your heart pumps an average of 1,500 gallons of blood every day. Throughout your lifetime, your heart will pump more than thirteen million oil barrels of blood.

You can determine your heartbeat by taking your pulse. Find the beat on your wrist or neck with your index and middle finger. Count the beats for exactly one minute. Do three trials to be sure you are accurate. Run or exercise for five minutes and check your pulse again. It should be much faster. Care for your heart, and it will give you a lifetime of service.

Check Your Understanding

1. What is the measure of your heartbeats in one minute?
   a. the lungs
   b. a contraction
   c. expansion
   d. a pulse

2. According to the passage, what is your likely heartbeat?
   a. 70 times a minute
   b. 78 times a minute
   c. 130 times a minute
   d. 85 to 90 times a minute

3. What can you infer about the dangers of breathing contaminated air based on how the heart pumps oxygen to the body?
   a. Contaminated air and smoking reduce the oxygen levels, and less oxygen will be pumped to the body.
   b. It doesn't matter what you breathe because you are young.
   c. Your body filters out the contamination so it doesn't matter.
   d. You aren't affected by smoke until you're forty.

4. What can you infer about the relationship between heartbeats and the age of healthy people?
   a. Heartbeats are higher in adults than in children.
   b. Heartbeats become lower between infancy and adulthood.
   c. Age doesn't affect pulse rates.
   d. both a and b

/4

Name ______________________________

Warm-Up 21

Cricket-Jumping Contests

Cricket-jumping contests are fun, and while participating in them, you can learn a lot about crickets! There are many species of crickets, but field crickets are common and easy to find. Because field crickets are **nocturnal**, it is best to collect them at night when they come out from their hiding places near rocks, wet dirt, and grass.

Although crickets have wings, they usually prefer to jump. Their powerful legs are their main source of protection. Male crickets "fiddle" more than they fly. They rub their wings together, and the "music" produced by this friction attracts females for mating. Crickets walk with two pairs of front legs, but they jump with a pair of long, rear legs. They have a pair of cerci that function like rear antennae. Each cercus has as many as 720 tiny bristles that detect movement in the air.

Once you've located a cricket, gently set it on the ground while a partner sets down his or her cricket. Use an area where you can estimate the length and height of the cricket's jump using a yardstick. Slap your hand on the ground behind the cricket. The cerci will feel the moving air, and the cricket will jump high and away from the danger it perceives. Give each cricket several trials before the cricket no longer reacts to the stimulus, or moving air. Happy jumping!

Check Your Understanding

1. How do the two cerci on the rear of the cricket warn the cricket of danger?
   a. They hear movement.
   b. They feel moving air and, thus, potential danger.
   c. They see enemies.
   d. They are used to sting enemies.
2. What do male crickets do with their wings?
   a. They talk to other crickets.
   b. They rub their wings together and make sounds to attract mates.
   c. They fight with other crickets.
   d. They jump with other crickets.
3. What is the main idea of the passage?
   a. how to get crickets to jump
   b. why crickets are nocturnal
   c. how to care for crickets
   d. why crickets sing
4. From the context of the passage, what is the meaning of **nocturnal**?
   a. active during the day
   b. active when it is wet
   c. active during bad weather
   d. active at night

/4

Warm-Up 22

Name ____________________

The Liberty Bell

The Liberty Bell was ordered from England in 1751 by the colony of Pennsylvania. The colonists wished to use it in their State House. When the bell arrived and was rung, it cracked. It was melted down and remade by local bell makers. The bell was then rung for many years. A message of freedom was engraved on the bell. It says, "Proclaim Liberty throughout all the land unto all the inhabitants thereof."

The bell was rung on important occasions. Pennsylvania colonists used the bell to express their anger over British taxes. They rang it to celebrate the Boston Tea Party. On July 8, 1776, it announced the first public reading of the Declaration of Independence. It was also rung when Chief Justice John Marshall died in 1835.

In the 1830s, abolitionists rang the bell as a symbol of liberty to oppose slavery. It then became known as the Liberty Bell. The bell was always rung each year to celebrate George Washington's birthday on February 22. When it was rung on his birthday in 1846, a long crack split the bell. After that, it was never rung again. The bell could no longer ring loudly, and people feared that it might split further apart. The Liberty Bell was taken out of the Pennsylvania State House and housed in the Liberty Bell Center in 2003.

Check Your Understanding

1. What caused the decision to stop ringing the Liberty Bell?
   a. The sound bothered people.
   b. The crack in the bell prevented the bell from ringing loudly.
   c. President Washington didn't want the bell rung any longer.
   d. It was moved to a different building.

2. Which of the following does the passage tell you about the abolitionists?
   a. They wanted to defeat Great Britain.
   b. They approved of Negro slavery.
   c. They opposed slavery.
   d. They wanted to abolish taxes.

3. What can you infer about the importance of George Washington to Americans in the first years after the founding of the United States?
   a. Washington was greatly admired and highly respected.
   b. Ringing the bell on Washington's birthday was symbolic of American liberty.
   c. Washington was largely forgotten.
   d. both a and b

4. What can you infer about Chief Justice John Marshall?
   a. He was greatly respected and important to Americans.
   b. He was president of the United States.
   c. People didn't like him.
   d. He had many enemies.

/4

Warm-Up 23

Name ______________________________

"Big Mama" Oviraptor

In the early 1990s, dinosaur hunters from the American Museum of Natural History in New York went on an expedition. They traveled to the Gobi Desert in central Asia. The leaders, Michael Novacek and Mark Norell, intended to explore the area where an earlier expedition had taken place. During this quest, scientists found dinosaur eggs and one of the largest dinosaur graveyards in the world. What they found stunned the world of *paleontology*, the science that studies fossils.

A nest discovered by Norell had a child-sized oviraptor in it. It was sitting on at least twenty eggs. The dinosaur's front limbs were wrapped around them. It appeared to be trying to protect the eggs in a devoted manner. Because of this, the scientists nicknamed her "Big Mama."

Had her eggs survived, this mother oviraptor probably would have hunted other small meat-eating dinosaurs to feed her young.

The dinosaur lived about seventy million years ago. It was likely killed by a fierce sandstorm or a collapsing sand dune. Over time, the soft tissues of the muscles, skin, and organs rotted away under layers of sand and sedimentary rock. Minerals from ground water seeped into the bones and eggs and fossilized them.

Check Your Understanding

1. What subject do paleontologists study?
   a. eggs
   b. living animals
   c. fossils
   d. people
2. From the context of the passage, what can you infer led to the nickname "Big Mama"?
   a. The mother probably fed other dinosaurs to its young.
   b. the protective position of the oviraptor
   c. the number of eggs
   d. both a and b
3. What likely killed "Big Mama"?
   a. a snowstorm
   b. a large dinosaur
   c. water
   d. a sandstorm or a collapsing sand dune
4. Which of the following pieces of information is *not* relevant to the discovery of the oviraptor?
   a. "Big Mama" carefully laid its eggs in a circle.
   b. It brought food for its young.
   c. Oviraptor means "egg thief."
   d. The bones were buried in sediment.

/4

Warm-Up 24

Name ______________________________

Birthday Odds

What are the **odds** that two of your classmates will share a birthday on the same month and day? Of course, if you had over 366 people in your class, the answer would be obvious! If they were the same age, they would share the same year, as well.

However, far fewer people are needed to have a very good chance of sharing the same birthday. The chances are **50-50**, or one in two, that two people will share the same birthday in any group of twenty-three people. So if your class has twenty-three or more students, the chances are quite good that two classmates will have the same birthday. A group of only fourteen people have a 50-50 chance of having two people with a birthday only one day apart. And in a group of only seven people, there is a 50-50 chance of having two people with birthdays only one week apart.

To test the odds, make a chart to see how many of your classmates have birthdays on the same day. Remember, you have one chance in two of finding the same days. The odds are better, of course, if you survey two or more classes. For fun, check with your extended family to see if anybody shares dates.

Check Your Understanding

1. What are the odds that two of your classmates will share a birthday if you have twenty-three people in your class?
   a. 50-50
   b. 1 in 10
   c. 2 in 3
   d. no chance
2. From the context of the passage, what is the best meaning of **odds**?
   a. unlikely to happen
   b. likely to occur
   c. certain to occur
   d. chances of happening
3. Based on the information in the passage, what are the odds of two members in a family of seven having a birthday a week apart from each other?
   a. The passage doesn't say.
   b. 50-50
   c. 1 in 10
   d. 2 in 7
4. From the context of the passage, what is the best meaning of **50-50**?
   a. one chance in 50
   b. one chance in two
   c. no chance of happening
   d. one half of two

/4

Name ______________________________

Warm-Up 25

Be a Better Speller

English has a lot of spelling irregularities because so many of our words have been borrowed from foreign languages. Others have developed from common usage by Americans with different dialects and unique expressions. There are some tricks and tips that will help you become a better speller. For example, students are often confused when *e* and *i* are next to each other. "Use *i* before *e* except after *c* or when sounded as *aye,* as in *neighbor* and *weigh.*" So *freight*, *reign*, and *vein* all have a long *a* sound and are spelled with "ei." Words with "cei" include *receive*, *deceive*, and *ceiling*. The long *e* sound is the opposite and includes such words as *yield*, *believe*, and *siege*. "When two vowels go walking, the first one does the talking." When there are two vowels in a row, the first one is the one sounded out, as in *stream* and *roast*. The only word that ends in "full" is *full*. All other words end in "ful," as in *thoughtful*, *fearful*, and *delightful*.

Other tips to help your spelling are to learn the correct spelling and meanings for simple homophones, such as *there* (over there), *their* (belonging to them), and *they're* ("they are"). Now that you are an expert speller, go try out for a spelling bee!

Check Your Understanding

1. Based on the information in the passage, which of the following words is spelled incorrectly?

a. siege
b. receive
c. successfull
d. sealed

2. Which of the following is a topic sentence?

a. first paragraph, last sentence
b. first paragraph, first sentence
c. second paragraph, first sentence
d. second paragraph, last sentence

3. Which of the following is an opinion and *not* a fact?

a. The English language borrows words from foreign languages.
b. Everyone should try out for a spelling bee.
c. Spelling rules are too challenging.
d. both b and c

4. Which of the following is *not* a homophone?

a. too
b. their
c. dog
d. him

/4

Warm-Up **26**

Name ______________________________

Frozen Food

Clarence Birdseye was a taxidermist. He stuffed dead animals for a living. However, what he really wanted to do was cook. He didn't just want to cook ordinary food. He wanted to be a chef. He enjoyed cooking fancy meals for his family. During a trip to the Arctic, Clarence watched Eskimos freeze fish and other meat in barrels of ice-cold, salty seawater. The water kept the food from spoiling. Clarence thoroughly investigated the process and inspected the stored fish. The meats and fish were thawed and used months later during the summer. He found that these foods retained all of their flavor and remained unspoiled.

When Clarence Birdseye got back home, he tried preserving different kinds of food using ice and brine (salt water). He was delighted to find that the process worked. He also invented a wax-lined cardboard box for storing frozen vegetables. One of the first vegetables he preserved was frozen spinach. He packed it in solid blocks using his lined boxes. The first frozen food was sold in Springfield, Massachusetts, and was called Birds Eye Frosted Foods®. Soon, Clarence put his name on an entire medley of frozen vegetables, and today frozen foods are common in every grocery store. His new occupation surely pleased Clarence more than taxidermy!

Check Your Understanding

1. Which of the following best describes a taxidermist?
   a. a frozen food specialist
   b. a person who freezes dead animals
   c. a person who stuffs dead animals to preserve them and make them look lifelike
   d. an Eskimo
2. What did Clarence Birdseye design to prevent water or food from leaking out of the frozen food package?
   a. a wax-lined box
   b. spinach
   c. salt water
   d. nothing
3. What is the main idea of the passage?
   a. how the Eskimos contributed to frozen food
   b. how Clarence Birdseye refined frozen food
   c. how taxidermy and frozen food are related
   d. the story of Clarence Birdseye
4. Which of the following events happened second?
   a. Clarence thoroughly investigated how to freeze food.
   b. Clarence watched the Eskimos preserve meat and fish.
   c. Clarence froze different kinds of food.
   d. Clarence invented the wax-lined box.

/4

Warm-Up 27

Name ______________________________

Checkers

Checkers is one of the oldest board games in the world. It was played by the Egyptians more than 3,000 years ago. It was very popular with the Egyptian kings, called pharaohs. The game is basically a war game. It involves strategy with long-term planning and tactics before each move. Historians who study earlier civilizations know it was popular because these kings always wanted their most precious possessions with them in their tombs. Checker sets have been found in the tombs of several of these Egyptian god-kings. They expected to play checkers when they were dead in the afterworld.

There are some differences between the ancient and modern game. Today, a checkerboard has sixty-four squares with alternating red and black colors. The ancient game usually had only fifty-two uncolored squares.

Historians are uncertain whether chess or checkers came first. They are both played on the same board. Checkers is considered a much easier game. There is far less strategy involved in playing. It is more likely that checkers preceded chess.

The game has other ancient roots besides Egypt. The ancient Greek poet Homer wrote *The Odyssey* nearly eight centuries before Christ. This long, famous poem about Odysseus describes how his wife refuses to believe her husband is dead. **Suitors** anxious to marry her played checkers while waiting for her to accept one of them.

More than 2,000 books have been written on the strategy of checkers. The game appeals equally to children and adults. Have you ever played it?

Check Your Understanding

1. According to the passage, which of the following statements is *not* true?
   a. Egyptian pharaohs played checkers.
   b. Checkers is equally popular with both adults and children.
   c. Homer played checkers with Odysseus.
   d. both a and b

2. A checkerboard today has
   a. fifty-two red and black squares.
   b. fifty-two uncolored squares.
   c. sixty-four uncolored squares.
   d. sixty-four red and black squares.

3. Which expression is similar to **suitors**?
   a. warriors
   b. men courting a woman
   c. kings
   d. men wearing suits

4. Which piece of information supports the idea that checkers is an ancient game?
   a. Many older people like to play checkers.
   b. Checker sets were found in the tombs of pharaohs.
   c. A checker tournament was held in 1905.
   d. The game appeals to children.

/4

Warm-Up 28

Name ______________________________

Author Roald Dahl

If you have heard of Whangdoodles, Snozzwangers, and the Pink-Spotted Scrunch, then you have probably read a book by Roald Dahl. This English author is one of the most popular writers for children. He has a **zany** sense of humor. He creates fascinating characters and unusual plots. Dahl wrote in a hut, like Willy Wonka's top-secret room. And he never allowed it to be dusted or even swept!

Dahl adored some of his characters. In fact, he would sometimes pretend to be the BFG, or "Big Friendly Giant," with an imaginary trumpet at his children's windows. Dahl clearly remembered his own childhood. He used characters like little Sophie in the *BFG* to show how it felt to be a child in an adult world. Dahl believed that if an adult wanted to know what it's like to live in a child's world, the grown-up should "get down on his hands and knees and live like that for a week."

This author of *Charlie and the Chocolate Factory* and *The Fantastic Mr. Fox* kept two thick idea books where he jotted down ideas for books and characters. Many of his books were suggested in these journals years before they were written. You may especially enjoy the nasty characters in his books, such as Miss Trunchbull and the Twits, as well as the aunts in *James and the Giant Peach*. What is your favorite Roald Dahl book?

Check Your Understanding

1. From the context of the passage, what is the meaning of **zany**?
   a. serious
   b. crazy and silly
   c. angry
   d. huge
2. A Dahl character who is nasty would be
   a. angry.
   b. crazy.
   c. both mean and ridiculous.
   d. very large.
3. Which word best describes the attitude of the writer toward Dahl in the passage?
   a. admiration
   b. hate
   c. disgust
   d. fury
4. What did Roald Dahl believe children's authors should do?
   a. get very serious
   b. write six hours a day
   c. give out chocolate
   d. learn to think and act like a child

/4

Warm-Up 29

Name ______________________________

Making Crayons

Crayons have been popular children's playthings for decades. Almost every child and adult enjoys the look, feel, and smell of new crayons. Crayons are made from three basic ingredients: pigment, paraffin, and stearic acid. Pigment is made from various chemicals mixed with water in mixing tanks. After it is completely mixed, the solution is filtered to remove water and scraped off the filter trays. It is baked in a kiln to dry it completely. Then it is ground into a fine powder, ready to be mixed with paraffin. Paraffin is a **by-product** of oil production. It is stored at the crayon factory in large, warm storage tanks. Warm, gloppy paraffin is sent through pipes into a vat where the pigment is added. Stearic acid, which gives crayons their distinctive crayon smell, is added to the mixture.

When the ingredients are thoroughly mixed, the solution is poured into trays with thousands of holes. Cold water is circulated to help the mixture cool quickly. A machine pushes the cooled crayons out of their holes. Expert crayon-checkers inspect each crayon to make sure it is perfect. The crayons are covered with glue and two labels to keep each crayon strong. They are funneled with other colors to make complete boxes of eight, sixteen, or sixty-four crayons. The next time you get a box of crayons, examine them, smell them, and then enjoy using them!

Check Your Understanding

1. Which of the following is used to make crayons?
   - a. paraffin
   - b. stearic acid
   - c. pigment
   - d. all of the above
2. From the context of the passage, what is the meaning of **by-product**?
   - a. something produced when another product is made
   - b. something you have to buy
   - c. something only used in making crayons
   - d. something made out of crayons
3. What causes crayons to have their distinctive smell?
   - a. paraffin
   - b. glue
   - c. pigment
   - d. stearic acid
4. Which comes last in the process of making crayons?
   - a. making the pigment
   - b. cooling the crayons
   - c. inspecting the crayons
   - d. adding stearic acid

/4

Warm-Up 30

Name ____________________

American Idioms

American English has a lot of unique expressions that come from the daily speech patterns of ordinary people. These sayings, which are unique to people and a language, are called *idioms*. The words mean something very different than the literal or exact meaning of each word. For example, if your mother says, "you got up on the wrong side of the bed," she really means that you're in a bad mood. If you buy something "for a song," you didn't literally sing for it, but what you bought was inexpensive.

If someone is "pulling your leg," he or she is trying to fool you. If your friend "sold you down the river," he or she betrayed you. When you are getting secrets "straight from the horse's mouth," you are getting the information from a reliable source. If you're "at the end of your rope," you can't handle the problem anymore. You may want to "knock their socks off" (impress) if you try out for a play. Your best friend will tell you not to "spill the beans" when telling you a secret he or she doesn't want anyone else to know. You will have to "bite the bullet" if you do something wrong and have to face the consequences. Don't "jump down your brother's throat" (scold severely) if you're angry with him. Just "take the bull by the horns" (be in control) and "stick to your guns" (keep your position) when you have to do a tough job.

Check Your Understanding

1. Which idiom means to face the consequences?
- a. "sold you down the river"
- b. "for a song"
- c. "bite the bullet"
- d. "at the end of your rope"

2. What is the meaning of the idiom "people in glass houses shouldn't throw stones"?
- a. Use wooden walls in a house.
- b. Don't accuse others of things you also do.
- c. Don't peek into people's homes.
- d. Be careful of glass.

3. If the "cat got your tongue," what is your real problem?
- a. You don't know what to say.
- b. You're afraid of cats.
- c. You're "up a creek without a paddle."
- d. You have too many cats in your house.

4. If you're "sitting pretty" and "feel like a million dollars," which phrase best describes your mood?
- a. sad and angry
- b. happy and comfortable
- c. in danger and in trouble
- d. lucky and upset

/4

Fascinating People

Warm-Up 1

Name ____________________

Beverly Cleary

Beverly Cleary didn't like learning to read in school. In fact, her first-grade teacher assigned her to the Blackbirds because she was having so much trouble. This was the lowest reading group. She lived on a farm near the small town of Yamhill, Oregon. Cleary had only two books at home: *Mother Goose* and *The Three Bears*. Her mother helped create the first library in town and became the town librarian. Eventually, Cleary grew up and attended college at Berkeley and the University of Washington. She became a librarian herself.

Ten years later, she started her first book. Beverly Cleary wanted to write books for children that she would have liked to read as a child. She finished *Henry Huggins* the same year it was accepted by a major publisher. In the years to follow, Beverly Cleary went on to create more stories. She wrote about the everyday adventures of Henry, his dog Ribsy, and a feisty girl named Ramona. They lived in a small Oregon town like she had growing up. Cleary's stories are usually peopled with ordinary children. They have to use their intelligence and courage to solve their problems. There is a little bit of Ramona in every child. Both boys and girls relate to her personal **quirks** and private worries.

Other books written by Cleary include *The Mouse and the Motorcycle* series. Another book, *Dear Mr. Henshaw*, won the Newbery Award as the best children's book of 1984. Have you ever read one of these books?

Check Your Understanding

1. Which reading group did Beverly Cleary belong to as a first-grader?
   a. the Bluebirds
   b. the Redbirds
   c. the Blackbirds
   d. the Hawks
2. Which of the following would be the best title for the passage?
   a. "From Blackbird to Bluebird"
   b. "The Creator of Henry and Ribsy"
   c. "An Author for Children"
   d. "Beverly Cleary: Her Life and Books"
3. From the context of the passage, what is the meaning of **quirks**?
   a. unusual personal traits
   b. mean actions
   c. bravery
   d. reading books
4. Which fact supports the proposition that Beverly Cleary is an excellent children's author?
   a. Cleary was from Oregon.
   b. She won a Newbery Award.
   c. She wrote a book in less than a year.
   d. both a and c

/4

Warm-Up 2

Name ____________________

He Mailed Himself to Freedom

Henry Brown was a Virginia slave who desperately wanted to be free. He knew that his only hope for freedom was to get across the border from Virginia to Maryland. From there, he hoped to get into Pennsylvania. He knew that if he ran away, though, slave catchers would have a good chance of catching him. He would be in a part of the country where he did not know his way around. Slave catchers were always near the state borders hunting for runaway slaves.

Henry decided on a much bolder escape. He decided to mail himself to freedom. He convinced a carpenter friend to build him a wooden box just barely large enough for him to squeeze into. He could sit folded up in the space. He hid himself inside the box with water, a few biscuits, and a small tool he used for drilling air holes. The box was nailed shut and shipped by train to Philadelphia. He often ended up riding upside down during the twenty-six-hour trip.

When the box was delivered to the Anti-Slavery Society of Philadelphia, the leaders opened it and Henry stepped out. He was a free man. Brown spoke at antislavery meetings and helped others escape along the Underground Railroad. He was even the subject of a song telling of his escape.

Check Your Understanding

1. Which of the following words describe Henry Brown's character and personality?
   a. courageous
   b. clever
   c. fearful
   d. both a and b
2. From the context of the passage, which of the following best describes the Underground Railroad?
   a. a subway from Virginia to Pennsylvania
   b. a system for helping slaves escape
   c. a mail train
   d. a group of slave catchers
3. What dangers did Henry Brown face during his trip to Pennsylvania?
   a. getting caught by the authorities in Virginia
   b. getting too fat on the trip
   c. getting sick because he ate too much
   d. none of the above
4. Which fact is essential to understanding Henry's decision to mail himself to Pennsylvania?
   a. Henry liked receiving mail.
   b. Henry was a slave in Virginia.
   c. Henry liked riding on trains.
   d. Henry's journey took twenty-six hours.

/4

Warm-Up 3

Name ____________________

Hypatia

Hypatia was the greatest female math and science teacher in the ancient world. She was educated to be a scholar by her father. He was a mathematics teacher at the great Library of Alexandria in Egypt. He had no sons. He decided to raise his daughter to be educated and strong in mind and body. He believed that if girls were given the chance, they could learn as well as boys. He also believed in physical exercise for girls.

Hypatia grew up to become a brilliant and beautiful young woman. She studied with a famous teacher in Athens for a time. This would be like going to college today. She returned home to become the first woman teacher at the Library of Alexandria. This was a library for writings from all over the ancient world. It was also a university for teaching and research in all subjects.

Hypatia became known for her writing about math ideas. She also invented an astrolabe and a planisphere for studying the stars. She developed a new method for distilling clean water, as well. She also taught her personal ideas, which took what she found best from all religious beliefs. Hypatia's teachings irritated a leader in the city. He arranged to have a mob attack her as she drove her chariot through the city. She was killed. However, nobody could kill her spirit. It lives on today as a model for young girls.

Check Your Understanding

1. What subject would a planisphere and an astrolabe be used to study?
   a. mathematics
   b. philosophy
   c. astronomy
   d. exercise

2. Which of the following best describes the Library of Alexandria?
   a. library
   b. university
   c. high school
   d. both a and b

3. Why was Hypatia murdered?
   a. She angered a city leader.
   b. She studied science.
   c. She studied mathematics.
   d. both a and b

4. Which word best describes Hypatia?
   a. teacher
   b. mathematician
   c. scientist
   d. all of the above

/4

Warm-Up 4

Name ____________________

The Secret Soldier

Because of her mother's illness, Deborah Sampson was sent to work as a servant for neighbors from the time she was eight until she turned eighteen. She was a strong supporter of General Washington and the idea of American independence from England. Sampson decided to sign up for the army. She put on men's clothing and cut her hair. Although she was worried about being discovered right away, Sampson enlisted in the army on May 20, 1782. She used a man's name, Robert Shurtleff. She was trained with the other soldiers. She went on long marches to fight the English. Like the other soldiers, she ate bad food and had poor clothing and supplies. "Robert" kept to herself and worked without complaining. She was trusted and popular with the other soldiers. Their nickname for her was "Blooming Bobby." They often teased her about her lack of a beard. They thought she had lied about her age and was a fifteen-year-old boy.

Sampson went on scouting missions looking for enemy supplies. She fought in many minor battles with enemy soldiers. During one small battle, she was wounded and dug the bullet out of her leg herself. She did not want to take a chance of her secret being discovered by a doctor. Later, Sampson caught a fever and nearly died. She lived, but her secret was discovered by a doctor. He informed her superior officer. Deborah Sampson was **honorably discharged** from the army on October 25, 1783, as the war was ending.

Check Your Understanding

1. From the context of the passage, what is the meaning of **honorably discharged**?

a. sent home
b. left the service with a good record
c. a fake name
d. thrown out for poor service

2. From reading the passage, what can you infer is the reason why Deborah Sampson was discharged from the army?

a. She was a woman and her secret was discovered.
b. She was needed back home.
c. She was too sick to fight.
d. She had been a poor soldier.

3. How can you tell that beards and facial hair were very common in the Continental army?

a. No one had razors.
b. George Washington wore a beard.
c. Soldiers without beards were teased and presumed to be very young.
d. Wearing a beard was required by the officers.

4. How long did Deborah Sampson serve in the American army?

a. two years
b. eight years
c. two and one-half years
d. one and one-half years

/4

Warm-Up 5

Name ____________________

The Most Important Woman in America

In the middle of the 1800s, Sarah J. Hale was the most important woman in America. She became the first woman editor in the nation. The magazine she edited was called *Godey's Lady's Book*. It had many articles on the latest fashions and the newest hairstyles. However, she also made it a magazine of ideas she believed were important for women. It became the most popular U.S. women's magazine for almost fifty years.

She used the pages of her magazine to urge six presidents to start an annual day of thanksgiving. She finally succeeded in 1863. That year, President Lincoln declared a day of prayer and thanksgiving. She made sure later presidents kept up the new holiday.

Hale was a firm defender of the rights of women and children. She wanted women to become teachers at a time when only one teacher in fifty was a woman. She was successful. When she retired from the magazine, most teachers were women. She also wanted teaching colleges that young women could attend. She opposed spanking for children in school. And she wanted women to serve on school boards. This was before women even had the right to vote.

Hale was a leader in building the first college for women. She also wrote to support the idea of building nurses' training colleges for young women. She believed that medical colleges should be opened for women doctors. She believed that women and children had special medical needs that women doctors would focus on. Before she became famous, Hale wrote books of children's poetry. Her most famous poem was "Mary Had a Little Lamb." Hale also wrote the first novel by a woman in the United States.

Check Your Understanding

1. Which of the following did Sarah Hale *not* support?
   a. women teachers in schools
   b. a national day of thanksgiving
   c. physical punishment for children in schools
   d. the education of women doctors

2. Which of the following did Hale *not* write?
   a. a novel
   b. children's poetry
   c. dictionaries
   d. magazine articles

3. Which of the following was probably *not* a reason Sarah Hale wanted a national day of thanksgiving?
   a. to bring families together in celebration
   b. to express gratitude for the nation's good fortune
   c. to have a day where everyone gives thanks
   d. to start the holiday shopping season

4. Why was *Godey's Lady's Book* important to Hale?
   a. It allowed her to publish and explain her opinions.
   b. She was able to advocate causes for women and children.
   c. She could campaign for a national day of thanksgiving.
   d. all of the above

/4

Warm-Up 6

Name ______________________________

Buffalo Bill Cody

Buffalo Bill Cody was one of the most famous men of the American West. After his father's death in Kansas, eleven-year-old Bill Cody got work carrying messages for a freight company. He then went on his first cattle drive to Salt Lake City, Utah. There, he was involved in his first conflict with American Indians. At fourteen, he became the "Boy Wonder" of the Pony Express. Once he made a twenty-two-mile round-trip ride in just twenty-one hours. It was a record never matched in the short history of that mail-carrying service. Cody joined the Union army during the Civil War. He served as a scout searching for enemy troop movements until the end of the war. Cody earned his nickname, "Buffalo Bill," by killing buffalo to feed the men laying track for the railroad. He was an excellent rifle shot, even at long distances. Later, Cody became the chief scout for the soldiers assigned to protect settlers on the plains. He was greatly admired by the American Indians he sometimes battled against because of his courage and honesty. They called him "Pahaska," which meant "long-haired." He was very proud of his long, blond hair. Buffalo Bill achieved his greatest fame as a showman in his Wild West Show. Famous frontiersmen like Wild Bill Hickok and Chief Sitting Bull performed in these shows. Annie Oakley showed off her **exceptional** shooting skills, as well. They drew huge crowds and many famous people. These visitors included presidents, kings, queens, and other famous people. This show was such a huge success that it continues today!

Check Your Understanding

1. From the following choices, which job is closest to that of a showman's?
   - a. an actor
   - b. a speaker
   - c. a scout
   - d. a soldier
2. Which side of the conflict in the Civil War did Buffalo Bill support and fight for?
   - a. British
   - b. Confederate
   - c. Union
   - d. neither
3. From the context of the passage, what is the meaning of **exceptional**?
   - a. unskilled
   - b. special
   - c. simple
   - d. average
4. Which of the following groups did Buffalo Bill *not* work for?
   - a. railroads
   - b. United States Army
   - c. Pony Express
   - d. Sioux Indians

/4

Warm-Up 7

Name ______________________________

"Eureka! I've Found It!"

Archimedes was one of the most important thinkers in world history. This Greek scientist, who lived about 2,300 years ago, was a student of science and mathematics, as well as all forms of learning. Archimedes studied spirals and circles and the idea of *pi*, a fraction used to find the area and distance around circles. He was one of the first scientists to use experimentation to test his ideas. He worked with simple machines and explored the uses of the lever. He explained the idea of the lever by saying, "Give me a place to stand, and I will move the Earth."

Archimedes was a close friend of the king of Sicily. The king asked him to determine if a gold crown he had ordered was completely gold or had cheaper metals in it. Archimedes was taking a bath when he discovered the answer. He realized that every metal on the crown displaced a different amount of water. The amount of water that moved was due to a metal's weight. He realized that water could be used to compare the specific weights of different metals. Archimedes was so **jubilant** at his discovery that he jumped out of his bath. He forgot his clothes and ran to the king's palace shouting, "Eureka!" which means, "I've found it!"

Archimedes also studied other properties of water, such as how objects floated. He developed a tool used to bring water uphill to dry areas of land. It is called the Archimedes screw. It was used to irrigate crops. It was based on his study of a kind of seashell with a spiral shape. Archimedes helped his king by designing war machines to fight off their Roman enemies. He was killed by a Roman soldier during a siege of his city, but his memory and discoveries live on.

Check Your Understanding

1. What can you infer about Archimedes' personality by reading the passage?
   a. He enjoyed making new discoveries.
   b. He was loyal to his king.
   c. He examined many things in nature and used his examinations to make new discoveries.
   d. all of the above

2. What is an Archimedes screw?
   a. a seashell
   b. a small tool for holding wood together
   c. a device for moving water uphill
   d. a war machine

3. From the context of the passage, what is the meaning of **jubilant**?
   a. rich
   b. extremely happy
   c. very depressed
   d. satisfied

4. Which of the following was a cause of Archimedes' discovery of the displacement of water by different metals?
   a. He studied conch shells.
   b. He took a bath with the crown.
   c. He studied levers.
   d. He studied circles.

/4

Warm-Up 8

Name ____________________

First Emperor of the United States

Joshua Norton settled in San Francisco in 1849. He was a rich man who grew even richer in those days of gold mining. Business was booming. However, Norton lost all of his money on a wild rice business that went broke. Norton's loss changed him. He dressed himself in an old military uniform and told the editor of the local newspaper of his new title and position as Norton I, Emperor of the United States. Maybe it was a slow news day or the editor was simply amused by the sheer **gall** of the man. In any event, he printed the story as a straight news item. The rest of the city went along with his game.

People spoke to Norton as "Your Majesty," and policemen saluted him. Norton issued statements about public affairs as if he were in charge of the country. In one statement, he abolished Congress. In another, he fired President Lincoln. Norton printed his own money, which was quickly bought up. Visitors bought the money as **souvenirs**. The emperor also taxed local businesses two or three dollars apiece. People were both amused by and fond of their emperor. When he died in 1880, 10,000 people filed past his casket. Norton was such an inspiration that he caught the attention of Mark Twain. The character of King in Twain's *The Adventures of Huckleberry Finn* is based on Norton. Norton may have been broke when he died, but he certainly made a difference while he lived.

Check Your Understanding

1. What was the most likely cause of Joshua Norton's decision to name himself emperor?
   a. He lost all of his money.
   b. He had been thinking about it for a long time.
   c. He wanted to run the country.
   d. The mayor needed help running San Francisco.
2. From the context of the passage, what is the best meaning of **gall**?
   a. emperor
   b. insanity
   c. fearfulness
   d. boldness
3. Which of the following events happened first?
   a. Joshua Norton declared himself emperor.
   b. Norton lost all of his money.
   c. Emperor Norton fired Abraham Lincoln.
   d. Norton printed his own money.
4. From the context of the passage, what is the meaning of **souvenir**?
   a. make-believe actions
   b. emperor
   c. something that is bought and kept to remember something or someone
   d. something that is buried

/4

Warm-Up **9**

Name ______________________________

Steven Spielberg

Steven Spielberg was born in December 1947. He was very imaginative as a young child. He liked dressing up in costumes and acting in plays he made up. In his teens, he used his dad's movie camera to make movies with friends. He even talked a local airport into letting him film scenes inside a real fighter plane. He won a junior film festival with a film he made in the Arizona desert using special effects. Spielberg was really a self-taught director. He submitted some of his films to Universal Studios. He dropped out of college because he was offered work at that studio. (He did finish college much later at California State University, Long Beach).

Spielberg's first film was called *Duel*. His first major success was *Jaws*, a scary movie about sharks. It made him popular and led to other successes. These included four *Indiana Jones* movies. They are filled with the adventures of a collector of ancient treasures. Another movie directed by Spielberg is *Jurassic Park*. It's about a dinosaur park. And *E.T.* tells the story of a creature from another world visiting earth.

Spielberg has also made some serious movies. *Schindler's List* tells the true story of one man's efforts to save Jews from the death camps during World War II. *Saving Private Ryan* is a story of a few soldiers trying to survive during that war. *The Color Purple* is a serious movie about the lives of African Americans.

In 1994, he joined with friends to start his own movie studio. It is called Dreamworks. In the same year, Spielberg provided money to record the stories of **survivors** of the death camps. He already has thousands of **oral** accounts recorded on videotapes.

What kind of movie do you hope Spielberg directs next—a drama, a comedy, or a romance?

Check Your Understanding

1. Which film did *not* deal with past periods of history?
   a. *Saving Private Ryan*
   b. *Jurassic Park*
   c. *Schindler's List*
   d. *E.T.*

2. Which of the following is based on a true story?
   a. *Schindler's List*
   b. *E.T.*
   c. *Saving Private Ryan*
   d. *Indiana Jones and the Temple of Doom*

3. From the context of the passage, what is the meaning of **oral**?
   a. written
   b. used for punishment
   c. spoken aloud
   d. not true

4. From the context of the passage, which of the following has the same meaning as **survivors**?
   a. people who are killed in an event
   b. leaders of people
   c. people who live through a terrible event
   d. lucky people

/4

Warm-Up 10

Name ______________________________

Galileo Galilei

Galileo was born about 350 years ago in Italy. More than any other scientist, he deserves to be considered the father of modern science. He was different from teachers before him and many in his own time. He tested each of his ideas with experiments and did very careful observations of the results. Other famous experts in science had based their opinions on ideas that had been stated for hundreds of years. Usually, the ideas had not been proven.

For example, Galileo was certain that light objects and heavy objects fall at the same speed. He thought an experiment would prove his belief. He tested his idea by dropping objects of different weights from a tower. He proved his idea. However, even that didn't convince some of his critics. He was also able to describe the speed of these falling objects in math terms. The use of math to describe scientific ideas was a major leap forward in science. He also described some laws of motion. He did major experiments with swinging pendulums, as well.

Galileo designed and built a telescope powerful enough to see the mountains and craters of the moon. He was able to see the first four moons of Jupiter. In his honor, they are called the Galilean moons. He was among the first to believe that Earth was not the center of the universe. He believed that the planets in the solar system revolved around the sun.

Galileo's ideas were advanced for his time. In many ways, he was too advanced to be appreciated, but now we appreciate him. Don't you wonder what ideas he would test if he were alive today?

Check Your Understanding

1. What are the Galilean moons?
   a. four moons around Saturn
   b. four moons of Jupiter first seen by Galileo
   c. four moons near the Sun
   d. four moons around Uranus first seen by Galileo

2. What does the passage suggest was believed by many other scientists of Galileo's time?
   a. Heavy objects fall faster than light objects.
   b. All planets and the sun revolve around Earth.
   c. Scientists should believe what earlier scientists had written.
   d. all of the above

3. Which of the following actions was an important scientific advance used by Galileo?
   a. discovering planets in the solar system
   b. inventing the first telescope
   c. looking at the moon
   d. expressing scientific observations with mathematical formulas

4. What can you infer about the influence of Galileo on scientists who succeeded him?
   a. They named the four moons of Jupiter after him because they respected his work.
   b. They ignored his efforts after he died.
   c. They continued his experiments immediately.
   d. They never used his telescope again.

/4

Warm-Up 11

Name ______________________________

One-Eyed Charley

One-Eyed Charley Parkhurst became a very famous stagecoach driver in the Old West. Charley left the tamer roads of the East. He made his **reputation** driving along the scary trails of California. The roads were often washed out by rain. They were filled with axle-breaking ruts and **bone-crunching** fallen stones. Even though he only had one eye due to a stagecoach accident, Charley always kept his vehicle on the road.

Outlaws were drawn to the gold carried in boxes on top of the stagecoach. They thought robbing it was an easy way to get rich. The first time Charley was held up along his route, he gave up the box without a word and left with the stagecoach and its passengers. The second robbery attempt was a different matter. When the masked bandit stepped into sight, Charley swept up his shotgun hidden on the seat. He shot the bandit in the chest and took off at high speed.

Charley soon became known as one of the toughest drivers on the California stagecoach routes. No one wanted to tangle with him. Hold-up men avoided him. However, One-Eyed Charley had one surprise left for everyone after he died. The doctor discovered that rough-tough, One-Eyed Charley was really a woman. She was also the first woman known to vote in California because, as a "man," she could vote. The children's book *Riding Freedom* by Pam Munoz Ryan tells Charley's exciting story.

Check Your Understanding

1. From the context of the passage, what is the meaning of **bone-crunching**?
   a. damaging
   b. one-eyed
   c. mean
   d. paved
2. What was Charley's last surprise?
   a. He was rich.
   b. He was a woman.
   c. He was afraid of bandits.
   d. He voted.
3. Which of the following sentences is a topic sentence?
   a. One-Eyed Charley Parkhurst became a very famous stagecoach driver in the Old West.
   b. Charley soon became known as one of the toughest drivers on the California stagecoach routes.
   c. No one wanted to tangle with him.
   d. both a and b
4. From the context of the passage, what is the meaning of **reputation**?
   a. how much a person is seen
   b. how much a person is trusted
   c. how much a person is afraid
   d. how much a person is valued by others

/4

Warm-Up 12

Name ______________________________

The Librarian Who Measured Earth

Eratosthenes was born about 2,240 years ago. He studied in the great centers of learning at the time. He became the director of the Library of Alexandria. He was a very successful scientist. He made many important discoveries. For example, he correctly measured the tilt of Earth's axis. In math, he developed a system for finding prime numbers. He also studied the movement of the planets. And he suggested the use of a leap year every four years. According to him, this would keep the calendar correct.

However, his greatest discovery was his ability to measure the distance around the center of Earth. He knew that Earth was round. He recognized this fact because he had seen the curved shadow of Earth during an eclipse. He knew that the sun cast no shadow on a deep well in a neighboring city. This was at exactly noon on the first day of summer.

Trained men measured the exact distance between the two cities. The librarian measured the arc of a circle formed by the two cities at 7.2 degrees. He then divided the 7.2 degrees into the 360 degrees of a circle. He realized that the distance around Earth was fifty times the distance between the two cities. In today's terms, that would be 25,000 miles. Little did he know, his **estimate** would be proven correct in modern times using exact measuring tools.

Check Your Understanding

1. How did Eratosthenes know that Earth was round?
   a. It looked round to him.
   b. An eclipse showed a curved shadow of Earth.
   c. The books said Earth was round.
   d. He used a telescope.

2. Which of the following is an accomplishment of Eratosthenes?
   a. a system for determining prime numbers
   b. measuring the tilt of Earth's axis
   c. measuring the distance around Earth
   d. all of the above

3. From the context of the passage, what is the best meaning of **estimate**?
   a. an unlikely guess
   b. the exact mathematical answer
   c. a close figure based on reasoning
   d. any number

4. Which sentence gives the main idea of the passage?
   a. the fourth sentence in paragraph one
   b. the second sentence in paragraph two
   c. the third sentence in paragraph one
   d. the first sentence in paragraph three

/4

Warm-Up 13

Name ______________________

Sir Walter Raleigh

Sir Walter Raleigh is probably best known as a knight in Queen Elizabeth I's court. He was the one who took off his red cape and laid it in the mud. He didn't want his queen to get her feet wet or her long dress dirty. This was a famous act of **chivalry** and added to his fame as a knight. It also increased his popularity with Elizabeth I. She enjoyed controlling the strong, handsome men who served her in court. They also fought for her in her conflicts with Spain and other countries.

Raleigh established a colony in the New World that he named Virginia in honor of Elizabeth's nickname. However, the first settlement in Virginia at Roanoke was abandoned, and the people disappeared. Raleigh served as captain of the Queen's guard for a time. He made a lot of money as a merchant sending ships to trade with other countries. He also sent a small fleet of pirates to rob Spanish ships. He searched in South America for a fabulous but **imaginary** City of Gold.

He got secretly married. This angered the queen. Elizabeth had Raleigh and his new wife imprisoned in the Tower of London. Raleigh later arranged their release from prison by writing poems praising the queen. He also gave her ships full of stolen Spanish treasure. Raleigh was not as successful with Elizabeth's successor, King James I. James didn't like Raleigh or trust him. James had Raleigh imprisoned in the Tower again for thirteen years. He ordered Raleigh's execution in 1618.

Check Your Understanding

1. From the context of the passage, what is the best meaning of **chivalry**?
   a. laying down clothes for a queen to walk on
   b. a code of honor and courtesy
   c. fighting with swords and spears
   d. a fear of fighting

2. Which of the following did Raleigh *not* accomplish?
   a. starting a permanent settlement in Virginia
   b. convincing Elizabeth to free him and his wife
   c. naming a colony in the New World
   d. capturing Spanish ships carrying gold

3. From the context of the passage, what is the meaning of **imaginary**?
   a. not real
   b. real
   c. queenly
   d. both b and c

4. Use the information in the passage to determine the most likely time of Sir Walter Raleigh's birth.
   a. about 1618
   b. about 1518
   c. about 1550
   d. about 1650

/4

Warm-Up 14

Name ______________________________

The One-Armed Explorer

John Wesley Powell lost most of his right arm when he was wounded in battle. Despite his injuries, he served three more years in the Union army. He was a major when the Civil War ended. As a young boy, Powell was thrilled by science. His personal collections of thousands of rocks and fossils led to his election as secretary of a natural history museum. During three separate trips, Powell rowed down the Mississippi, Ohio, and Illinois Rivers. Each time he collected "treasures" along the way. After the war, he taught **geology**.

In 1869, Powell decided to explore the last unmapped area in the United States. This was the area bordered by the Colorado River. It included the Grand Canyon. It was then called the "Great Unknown." With nine experienced outdoorsmen, Powell explored more than 1,000 miles of the river and canyon. He gathered rock samples. Some of them were more than two billion years old.

The expedition cost the lives of three explorers. One of the boats was destroyed, as well. They were out of supplies and near starvation when they finally reached safety. However, it was one of the greatest journeys in the history of science and exploration. In fact, it was so successful that it led to a second expedition.

Powell's advanced work in geology led to a new career in government. In March 1881, he became the director of the U.S. Geological Survey. This was a job he kept for thirteen years.

Check Your Understanding

1. Which of the following statements is an opinion and *not* a fact?
   a. The expedition led by Major Powell lost three explorers and one boat.
   b. Major Powell was the greatest explorer in American history.
   c. John Wesley Powell was a Union soldier.
   d. Powell was a student of fossils and geology.
2. Which of the following would be another good title for the passage?
   a. "The Man Who Explored the Grand Canyon"
   b. "Collecting Fossils"
   c. "John Wesley Powell: Fighting Soldier"
   d. "Union Soldier Loses Arm"
3. From the context of the passage, what is the meaning of **geology**?
   a. the study of rivers
   b. the study of water
   c. the study of rocks
   d. the study of living things
4. What can you conclude about the character of J. W. Powell?
   a. He was fearful and timid.
   b. He was determined, resourceful, and brave.
   c. He only learned from books.
   d. He was easy to work with.

/4

Warm-Up 15

Name ______________________________

Isaac Newton: Genius at Work

Isaac Newton was an **innovator**. He was born in 1642, and he died in 1727. In his life, he made some of the most important discoveries in the history of science. He completely changed the way Earth and the entire universe were understood by scientists. At the age of twenty-three, Newton discovered a major concept in algebra, which was then a new kind of math. At the same age, he worked out the basic ideas of calculus. This is a kind of math important to space travel and to understanding the size and nature of space. We couldn't even put a person in space without the figures made possible by this kind of math!

Newton also discovered the basic law of gravity. This is the idea that all objects in the universe are pulled toward each other. It explains that the strength of this pull depends on the size of each object. The force also depends on how far away objects are from each other. Heavier objects have greater power to pull other objects. And objects closer to each other have a greater power to pull. Newton explained the three laws of motion. These laws describe the actions of moving objects and how other forces affect these objects. All of his ideas help explain the nature of matter and energy.

Newton was the first scientist to prove that white light itself is made up of seven colors. They are red, orange, yellow, green-blue, violet, and indigo. He also invented the reflecting telescope. This improved tool made possible a much more detailed study of the stars and planets. In the minds of many people, Isaac Newton is the greatest scientist of all time.

Check Your Understanding

1. From the context of the passage, what does **innovator** mean?
   a. someone who plays with objects
   b. someone who studies colors
   c. someone who likes math
   d. someone who makes changes

2. Which of the following would be the most likely use of calculus?
   a. to compute the interest owed on a small debt
   b. to determine the amount of force needed to escape Earth's atmosphere in a rocket
   c. to compute the amount of gas needed to travel 500 miles in a car
   d. both b and c

3. Which of the following statements can you infer relate to the laws of motion?
   a. An unmoving object will remain unmoving until acted upon by an outside force.
   b. A moving object may speed up or slow down depending upon the force applied to the object.
   c. How much an object is affected by a force will depend upon the size and weight of the object.
   d. all of the above

4. Which of the following discoveries by Newton do not relate in some way to space, the universe, or planets?
   a. the law of gravity
   b. calculus
   c. laws of motion
   d. none of the above

/4

Warm-Up 16

Name ______________________________

Alexander the Great

Alexander the Great was born more than 2,300 years ago. In his teens, Alexander was taught by the most famous Greek teacher of his time, Aristotle. While still a youth, Alexander tamed a wild horse that only he was able to ride. He later rode that horse into battle for more than eighteen years. Alexander spent his teen years learning the skills of warfare and leadership.

When he was twenty, his father was murdered. The army chose Alexander as their leader. He went to war and defeated several Greek cities. He soon brought all of Greece under his control. Alexander then began a long series of battles against the Persian Empire. This empire was ruled by King Darius. Alexander had an army of more than 32,000 foot soldiers. He also had about 5,000 mounted horse soldiers. He defeated Darius in a major battle, but the king escaped.

Alexander then traveled to Egypt. He was crowned as a pharaoh, or god-king, by the Egyptians. They were grateful to get rid of their Persian rulers. He founded the city of Alexandria in that country. It would become one of their greatest cities. He returned to Persia and defeated Darius again. This time, Alexander captured over 7,000 tons of treasure. He used it to pay the costs of all of his future battles. He later traveled through many lands to the mountains, which were the gateway to India. He won several battles there and even fought against armies that used elephants like tanks. Alexander died of unknown causes when he was thirty-two years old. Some say it was malaria or typhoid fever. Others say he was poisoned. In any case, he will always be remembered for the life he lived—as one of the greatest commanders of all time.

Check Your Understanding

1. Which is the best description of Alexandria being founded?
   a. It was started, built, and named after Alexander.
   b. A city got renamed.
   c. The lost city got found.
   d. Alexander found a missing city.

2. Why was Alexander honored by the Egyptians and made a pharaoh?
   a. They didn't like the Persians who ruled Egypt.
   b. They needed a new pharaoh because one had died.
   c. Alexander seemed like a gentle king.
   d. Alexander named a city after himself.

3. How was Alexander educated as a young boy?
   a. He was taught by a famous teacher.
   b. He learned military skills.
   c. He didn't have to study anything.
   d. both a and b

4. How were Alexander's battles paid for?
   a. with credit cards
   b. with stolen treasure
   c. with horses and elephants
   d. both b and c

/4

Warm-Up 17

Name ______________________________

Sir Francis Drake

Francis Drake was born about 1540 in England. He became a young trainee aboard a trading ship at age thirteen. He made his first voyage to the New World when he was about twenty-five years old. The commander of this fleet of ships was a relative. Drake soon became a captain and became involved in sea battles with the Spanish. He lost his first battles with those ships. However, in the 1570s, Drake attacked Spanish ships and ports all over the New World. He took all of the treasure from the captured ships and ports. His group of pirate ships captured huge supplies of gold and silver. Drake gave a large part of the treasure to Queen Elizabeth I, and she made him a knight and a member of her court.

In 1577, Elizabeth chose Drake to lead a voyage around the world. During the course of this trip, Drake sailed across the Atlantic Ocean, around South America, and up the western coast of North America. He then sailed across the Pacific Ocean to Asia. He traveled around Africa and went home again to England. He became the first Englishman to sail around the world and return home.

After more battles with the Spanish, Elizabeth ordered Drake to destroy the Spanish **fleet** of 150 warships and 19,000 soldiers. The king of Spain put together this force to attack and defeat England. Using great skill and some good luck, Drake defeated and destroyed this Spanish fleet in 1588. It was an **epic** sea victory, and it made England the greatest military power in the world. Drake died in 1596 doing what he loved—fighting at sea.

Check Your Understanding

1. From the context of the passage, what is the meaning of **epic**?
   a. very big or impressive
   b. disappointing
   c. tired
   d. noisy

2. From the context of the passage, what is the meaning of **fleet**?
   a. a group of warships
   b. a group of Spanish trading vessels
   c. some pirates
   d. two ships

3. Who knighted Sir Francis Drake for his victories at sea?
   a. the king of Spain
   b. Queen Elizabeth II
   c. Queen Elizabeth I
   d. his sailors

4. Which statement would *not* be relevant to Drake's defeat of the Spanish fleet?
   a. The Spanish ships caught on fire and burned.
   b. Drake's attack disorganized the commanders of the Armada.
   c. Drake had sailed around the world.
   d. Drake was very lucky that the Spanish ships were waiting so close to each other.

/4

Warm-Up 18

Name ____________________

Claude Monet

Many painters are popular for a time. A few change art forever. In the mid-1800s, Claude Monet helped create an entirely new style of painting called Impressionism. This style has remained popular, not only in his lifetime, but even today. He and his friends in the Impressionist movement often left the **stuffy** studios where traditional painters worked and painted outside near the subjects that interested them. They even painted in rainy or windy conditions. Monet was especially interested in painting pictures of water, boats, oceans, lakes, and ponds. He equipped a boat as a floating studio and sailed along streams while painting subjects that attracted him. He enjoyed showing the way colors reflect in water and how water affects the clouds and sky.

Many of his paintings show people enjoying gardens. In one scene, he painted four young women in a garden. He used his favorite model, Camille, for all four girls. He later married her. He liked to paint the same subjects, such as a church or a country scene, at different hours of the day. The name for his style of painting came from one of his works called *Impression: Sunrise*. Over time, art lovers learned to enjoy this new style of art. Many people bought paintings from Monet and his friends. Monet spent the last years of his life painting scenes from his water garden. He died at age eighty-six. He had a long career as a popular and successful artist.

Check Your Understanding

1. From where did the name of the Impressionist art movement come?
   a. a painter
   b. one of Monet's paintings
   c. a kind of paint
   d. a boat

2. Which of these scenes would *not* appeal to Monet?
   a. a river
   b. a garden when it's raining
   c. an outdoor party
   d. a dark bedroom

3. Which statement is the best summary of the passage?
   a. Monet and his friends in the Impressionist movement changed the style and subjects of painting in a major way.
   b. Monet liked to paint gardens and flowers.
   c. Monet liked to paint on boats.
   d. Monet liked to use his wife as a model.

4. From the context of the passage, which is the best synonym for **stuffy**?
   a. fresh
   b. airy
   c. open
   d. closed-up

/4

Warm-Up 19

Name ______________________________

Steve Jobs

Steve Jobs had a lot of imagination and curiosity as a child. He enjoyed making spy movies at home with his friends in the neighborhood. His curiosity led him to do dangerous things, like stick a metal hairpin into an electric socket. (He was badly burned!) He also drank ant poison and had to have his stomach pumped at the hospital. He was not very well behaved in school and often wasted time. He was interested in anything scientific. He worked on inventions, took apart machines to see how they worked, and combined chemicals.

Jobs had few friends and didn't like school until he met Steve "The Woz" Wozniak. They met in high school. Woz was a whiz with electronics and was always inventing new **gadgets**. Jobs and Woz spent a lot of time building gadgets. Jobs even called the owner of a computer company to get some free parts. What he got was a good summer job building computers.

After a short stint at college and a job working with Atari®, Jobs and Woz created their own business. They worked out of Jobs's family garage. They named the company after a happy summer Jobs had spent picking apples in Oregon. They called it Apple Computers®. They created the Apple I Computer®, which was a success. They soon created a better version, the Apple II®, which was also successful. By the time he was twenty-five, Jobs was already worth over 250 million dollars. He would go on to make the Macintosh®. He would continue to develop computers and the products that use them, such as the iPod® and iPhone®. Steve Jobs, who passed away in October 2011, is considered one of the most inventive and successful businessmen of all time.

Check Your Understanding

1. How did Steve Jobs name his computer company?
   a. after his favorite apple
   b. after a memory of a happy summer job in Oregon
   c. after his best friend
   d. in honor of his mother

2. From the context of the passage, what is a **gadget**?
   a. something mechanical created to do a job
   b. a kind of computer
   c. a computer expert
   d. a college class

3. Which happened second in Jobs's life?
   a. He met Woz, and they became friends.
   b. He worked one summer for Atari.
   c. He invented the Apple II.
   d. He made spy movies at home.

4. Which of the following facts is *not* relevant to the career of Steve Jobs?
   a. He built the Apple I Computer in a box.
   b. They introduced the Apple II in 1977.
   c. Steve Jobs was sent to Germany by Atari to solve a problem.
   d. As a kid, Steve Jobs had to have his stomach pumped at the hospital.

/4

Warm-Up 20

Name ______________________________

Oprah Winfrey

Oprah Winfrey was born in 1954 in a small town in central Mississippi. She was the great-granddaughter of slaves. Her father was a soldier. Her mother was an eighteen-year-old girl who had no job. Oprah grew up with her grandmother until she was six. Then her grandmother became ill. She joined her mother in Milwaukee, but she eventually went to live with her father in Nashville. There, she finished high school and entered college.

Oprah got a job reporting news on the radio. She later reported the news on television in Nashville. For several years, she was a news reporter at a television station in Baltimore. Oprah got her big break in Chicago in 1984. There she hosted a morning program that soon became the *Oprah Winfrey Show*. Her program became a national show in 1986. She was also an actress in *The Color Purple*. She was nominated for an Academy Award for her role in the movie. Oprah's TV show also received several Emmy awards. She set up her own production company and, in 1988, became the owner of the show.

In 1995, Oprah was named on the Forbes list of the four hundred richest Americans. She was the only African American on the list. She started Oprah's Book Club. She produced and starred in the film *Beloved*. Two years later, Oprah started her own magazine. In 2002, she created a leadership **academy** for girls in South Africa. Now she has her own cable network. It is quite a success story for a girl born into poverty.

Check Your Understanding

1. From the context of the passage, which is the best synonym for **academy**?
   a. a poor school
   b. a school with high expectations for students
   c. a university
   d. a house

2. Which of the following did Oprah *not* produce or act in?
   a. *Beloved*
   b. *The Color Purple*
   c. *The Oprah Winfrey Show*
   d. the Forbes list

3. In which city did Oprah get her first job in broadcasting?
   a. Nashville
   b. Baltimore
   c. Chicago
   d. Milwaukee

4. From the context of the passage, what can you infer about Oprah's grandmother?
   a. She was well loved but unhappy.
   b. She was energetic and healthy.
   c. She was sick but kind.
   d. She was selfish and mean.

/4

Warm-Up
21

Name ______________________________

Dizzy Dean

In the 1930s, "Dizzy" Dean and his younger brother, Paul, were great pitchers for the St. Louis Cardinals. Dizzy became a radio and television broadcaster for twenty years after injuries shortened his playing career. Dean's unusual use of words made him popular and much quoted, except probably by English teachers.

Dizzy was very confident as a player. He tended to brag about his successes on the field. When he pitched a one-hitter and his brother pitched a no-hitter in a double header, he remarked, "If I had known what Paul was gonna do, I would have pitched one too." He once claimed, "If Satch [Satchel Paige] and I were pitching on the same team, we'd clinch the pennant by July 4 and go fishing until World Series time." He teased one batter, "Son, what kind of pitch would you like to miss?"

Dizzy rattled English teachers with his comments. He said " . . . there is a lot of people in the United States who say 'isn't', and they ain't eating." He also enjoyed stretching the truth with some inventive stories. After he gave several different hometowns in different states as his place of birth, he told the writers, "Them ain't lies; them's scoops." Another time, he remarked of a rather slow player, "He runs too long in one place. He's got a lot of up and down, but not much forward." The entire country laughed with Dean when he left a hospital after being hit on the head. He told the reporters, "The doctors X-rayed my head and found nothing."

Check Your Understanding

1. What are some of the English errors that Dizzy Dean made?
   a. using "ain't"
   b. using "them" instead of "they"
   c. using "there is" instead of "there are"
   d. all of the above

2. What does "unusual use of words" mean?
   a. creative expressions
   b. speaking a foreign language
   c. using an accent
   d. speaking perfectly

3. Which paragraph quotes several of Dizzy Dean's imaginative exaggerations?
   a. paragraph one
   b. paragraph two
   c. paragraph three
   d. both paragraph two and three

4. Which of the following information would *not* be relevant to support the main ideas of the passage?
   a. Dean was playing during a time of severe economic depression.
   b. Dizzy Dean won thirty games and lost seven in 1934.
   c. Dean once said, "It ain't bragging if you can do it."
   d. Dean once cleaned horse corrals as a child.

/4

Warm-Up 22

Name ______________________________

Michael Jordan

Michael Jordan is regarded by many as the greatest basketball player in the history of the game. He played the guard and forward positions. Jordan was famous for his accurate shooting in pressure situations and his exciting style of play. He could break loose from a crowd of players. Then he would drive over, around, and through the other players on the court to score. He was known for his "hang time." He seemed able to stay suspended in the air while making a driving layup or a long jump shot.

Michael Jordan was born in New York City and grew up in North Carolina. He did not show much early promise as a basketball player. He didn't even make his high school team as a freshman. He improved his game enough to be selected by the University of North Carolina. He made the winning shot in the final championship game of the NCAA tournament his freshman year.

Jordan was selected to play by the Chicago Bulls in the NBA. He was Rookie of the Year in the NBA in 1985. He led the Bulls to six NBA titles in the 1990s. In those years, he simply dominated the game. He had the highest average points per game for his entire career. He led the NBA in scoring in ten different seasons. Jordan left the Bulls in 1993 to play baseball, which didn't work out. He returned to the Bulls in 1995. Later, he was part owner and president of the Washington Wizards. He also played for them. He retired in 2003. Jordan was very successful in using his name to promote products, such as tennis shoes and sportswear. The popular Nike Air Jordan® shoes are named after him. His **endorsements** of these products remain successful even though he has retired from basketball.

Check Your Understanding

1. What is the best summary of the passage?
   a. Michael Jordan was a good basketball player.
   b. Jordan led the Chicago Bulls to six titles in the 1990s.
   c. Michael Jordan is perhaps the best basketball player in history.
   d. Michael Jordan made a lot of money on endorsements.

2. From the context of the passage, what is the best meaning of **endorsements**?
   a. selling products
   b. putting your name on and reputation behind a product
   c. supporting a friend
   d. playing forward in basketball

3. What is the author's purpose in writing the passage?
   a. to inform the reader
   b. to encourage the reader to play basketball
   c. to tell a story
   d. to make the reader laugh

4. Which of the following facts is *not* relevant to an article about Michael Jordan?
   a. Michael Jordan is six feet, six inches tall.
   b. Jordan played basketball in the Chicago Bulls organization.
   c. Jordan was MVP six times in the NBA finals.
   d. Karl Malone played in the NBA.

/4

Warm-Up 23

Name ______________________________

Eliza Harris

Eliza Harris was a young slave mother living in Kentucky. Two of her children had already died from starvation and mistreatment. She learned that she and her two-year-old daughter were to be sold to different owners. They would be separated from each other and from the rest of her children. Eliza fled. She was determined to get across the Ohio River to a free state. Then she intended to escape all the way north to Canada. Eliza walked many miles through the bitter cold of a winter night to the river. She carried her daughter in her arms. With slave catchers following close behind her, Eliza leapt onto a piece of ice floating down the river. She jumped to another chunk of ice when that piece started to break apart and sink.

Eliza crossed the wide river, jumping barefoot across broken ice pieces. She was still holding her child in her arms. A stranger who watched her **daring** crossing guided Eliza to a house. The house belonged to a family who helped African Americans escape from slavery. There were many people in the area that opposed slavery, and some of them helped runaways. She was then led to the homes of other people who moved her along secret routes to freedom. Eventually, Eliza returned and led her other children to freedom. Her story and name were later used in a novel against slavery, *Uncle Tom's Cabin*. In this way, her brave journey and strong character have been preserved for many years to come.

Check Your Understanding

1. From the context of the passage, what is the meaning of **daring**?

a. well-known and important
b. unknown
c. famous
d. brave

2. What do you think made the stranger want to help Eliza?

a. He had nothing else to do.
b. He was impressed by her courage crossing the river.
c. He wanted a reward.
d. He liked to walk.

3. How did Eliza show determination and courage in her escape?

a. She leaped barefoot from ice piece to ice piece while carrying her daughter.
b. She was being chased by slave catchers and that didn't stop her.
c. She didn't quit despite the pain and dangers.
d. all of the above

4. Who helped Eliza escape from Kentucky to Canada?

a. people opposed to slavery
b. Eliza's owner
c. slave catchers
d. her children

/4

Warm-Up 24

Name ______________________________

Nelson Mandela

Nelson Mandela became one of the best-known people in the world while he was in a prison cell. He spent twenty-seven years in prison. The leaders of South Africa wanted to keep blacks as second-class citizens. They put Mandela in prison because he publicly opposed their policy called **apartheid**. This policy forced all blacks to carry a passbook if they left home to go to another area. It was a way of controlling the movements of all blacks. Mandela publicly burned his passbook after the police shot sixty-nine blacks. They had gathered to peacefully protest against passbooks and forced separation. Blacks were kept separate from whites in all public areas and services. They had to live in different towns. They had to use different restaurants, schools, and even movie theaters.

In 1963, Mandela was arrested and accused of organizing a rebellion against the government. They said he was planning to destroy power lines, buildings, and public services. He was sent to prison for life. Mandela was kept in a cramped cell. He could receive only one visitor and one letter every six months. He had to dig in a lime pit or crush stones into gravel all day long. He soon became a leader among the prisoners. He protested the **mistreatment** of the men in jail and the mistreatment of blacks in the country.

Mandela became a symbol of freedom. He wanted the government to share power between blacks and whites. Other nations began to oppose the government. They refused to do business with South Africa. The leaders in his country realized that Mandela had to be released from prison. When he was freed, he received the Nobel Prize for Peace. He was soon elected as the new president of South Africa. Nelson Mandela has become a symbol of liberty to the world.

Check Your Understanding

1. From the context of the passage, what is the best meaning of **apartheid**?
- a. the separation of black people and white people
- b. a revolution against the government
- c. putting people in prison
- d. sharing power with both races

2. Which fact would support the proposition that Nelson Mandela was a good leader?
- a. He was always punctual, or on time.
- b. He refused to encourage violence against whites.
- c. He loves listening to classical music.
- d. While in prison, he worked in a gravel pit.

3. From the context of the passage, which is the best synonym for **mistreatment**?
- a. kindness
- b. cruelty
- c. running away
- d. bad feelings

4. Which of the following is an opinion and *not* a fact?
- a. Nelson Mandela was elected in 1994 to be president of South Africa.
- b. Mandela has been married three times.
- c. The apartheid laws began in 1948.
- d. Nelson Mandela was the most important leader in the world.

/4

Warm-Up 25

Name ______________________________

Louis Braille

Louis Braille was the three-year-old son of a French leather worker when he accidentally stabbed himself in the left eye. He was trying to push a sharp, pointed awl through a piece of leather in his father's shop. His parents stopped the bleeding and took him to a doctor. However, in 1812, even doctors did not yet know about germs. Louis got an infection in his injured eye, and it spread to his good eye. Within two years, Louis lost all of his sight and was permanently blind. Despite his blindness, his family helped him learn the places where he was walking. They taught him to recognize the voices of neighbors. His sister taught him to identify letters made of straw when he touched them. He was even allowed to attend the village school. He learned math very quickly and remembered everything the teacher said.

In 1819, Louis went to the first school for the blind in Paris, France. He would spend the rest of his life there. By the age of fourteen, Louis had read all fourteen of the Institute's raised letter books. He realized that a new code was needed to allow blind students to read with their fingers. He experimented with several codes using raised dots. He worked every night with a **stylus,** punching holes in paper. Within three years, he developed the Braille system, named in his honor by the other students. It took Louis twenty years to have his own system accepted. The authorities at the Institute first destroyed many of his books. Today, Braille is the most popular reading method for the blind.

Check Your Understanding

1. From the context of the passage, when was Louis Braille born?
   a. 1809
   b. 1812
   c. 1814
   d. 1819

2. How long did it take Louis to invent a system of writing for the blind?
   a. three years
   b. twenty years
   c. one year
   d. fourteen years

3. What led to Louis Braille's blindness?
   a. stabbing himself with an awl
   b. an eye infection
   c. a bee sting
   d. both a and b

4. From the context of the passage, what is a **stylus**?
   a. a tool for reading
   b. a tool for punching holes
   c. a new dance
   d. both a and b

/4

Warm-Up **26**

Name ______________________________

Julius Caesar

Julius Caesar was born about 2,100 years ago. Rome had become a hotbed of violence and political unrest. Corrupt groups and dishonest leaders within the ruling class fought each other to gain power. They did not care what it cost the people or the country. Caesar survived many conflicts within the brutal political battles in Rome. He made a temporary deal with the wealthiest man in Rome named Crassus. He also connected with the most famous general named Pompey. Caesar was the man in charge of pleasing the people in the city. Later, Caesar was made governor of Gaul, part of which today is France. He defeated the Gauls in an epic eight-year war. It cost the Gauls one million lives. Another one million people were sold into slavery.

Crassus died in a war. After his victories in Gaul, Caesar challenged Pompey for control of Rome. He captured Italy in a brilliant military campaign. He finally faced and defeated Pompey's army in Greece. He won a total victory. Pompey escaped and was killed in Egypt. Caesar became involved in plans to control Egypt. He formed a personal and political friendship with Cleopatra, the last queen of Egypt. He soon brought Egypt under the control of Rome.

Caesar returned to Rome where he made himself absolute **dictator**. This outraged the other members of the government. He was the only power in the country. A group of more than sixty men planned to kill him. Some were his friends. They believed that he had become too powerful. Caesar was stabbed to death in the Roman Senate on March 15, 44 BCE.

Julius Caesar had totally reformed Roman life. He brought about a number of changes in Roman law and government. He had also greatly extended the Roman Empire.

Check Your Understanding

1. From the context of the passage, what is a **dictator**?
   a. a soldier
   b. an empire
   c. a ruler with total power
   d. an army

2. What led to Pompey escaping to Egypt?
   a. He lost a battle in Egypt.
   b. He lost a battle in Greece.
   c. He lost a battle in Venice.
   d. both a and b

3. Which word means "military or political planning and actions"?
   a. campaign
   b. empire
   c. absolute
   d. hotbed

4. Which sentence is irrelevant to the information in the passage?
   a. Pompey had never been defeated in battle before his battle with Caesar.
   b. Crassus was a powerful Roman politician who had important political connections.
   c. Caesar was a Roman consul, the most important leader in Rome.
   d. Cleopatra was the last queen of Egypt.

/4

Warm-Up 27

Name ______________________

Bill Gates

Bill Gates was a good student in school, but he was more interested in a new invention. The personal computer was beginning to interest people in the early 1970s, and he was one of these people. By the age of fifteen, most of his classmates were playing sports and beginning high school. Bill Gates was working with computers. That year, Gates and a classmate, Paul Allen, set up their first software company. They wrote programs for computers. At the age of twenty, he and Allen began to design programs to run on PCs. They also started Microsoft® that year. Five years later, Microsoft was chosen by IBM® to design the operating system on their new PC. The operating system is the main program for running a computer's functions.

Bill was not yet thirty, and he was running one of the most vital new companies in the world. Gates wrote the system for running the IBM® and similar PCs. His company sold millions of copies. In 1985, Microsoft wrote the first **version** of the Windows® system. It is used on many computers. The company has sold millions of copies of Windows. It is constantly being revised and improved.

Bill Gates is still involved in making his company the leading maker of software for computers. However, he no longer runs the daily operations of his company. He still plans and develops new and better software. The success of his company has made Bill Gates one of the richest men in the world. But he doesn't keep his money for himself. He gives a lot to charity. He has created one of the largest charities. This charity supports efforts to improve health, education, and libraries all over the world. Gates has given billions of dollars so people can learn better and live longer.

Check Your Understanding

1. From the context of the passage, what is IBM?

a. a software company
b. a PC
c. a maker of personal computers
d. a company owned by Gates

2. From the context of the passage, what is the meaning of **version**?

a. a form of something
b. a charity
c. the final copy of a file
d. a story

3. What is the operating system of a computer?

a. the insides of a computer
b. the main program for controlling a computer's functions
c. the "on" switch
d. the maker of software

4. How old was Gates when Microsoft was chosen to develop the operating system for IBM personal computers?

a. fifteen
b. twenty-five
c. thirty
d. fifty

/4

Warm-Up 28

Name ____________________

Leonardo Da Vinci

Leonardo Da Vinci, born in 1452, was one of the most unusual men who ever lived. He was a genius in many fields of learning. He was born in Vinci, a small community in Italy. He studied art in Florence. Leonardo worked in Florence and Milan as an artist and a sculptor. He worked for powerful **dukes** controlling those cities. He also designed special stage shows using machines that he designed and built.

Leonardo planned many projects that he did not finish. These included a bronze horse that was used for weapons practice by soldiers. Da Vinci worked on the *Mona Lisa*, his most famous painting, for many years, but it was never completed. However, the rather hard-to-read smile on the woman's face is one of the most famous images in the history of art. Leonardo spent the last three years of his life at the castle of his last patron, the king of France. He died there in 1519.

Leonardo often studied the flight of birds. He used these studies to make designs for flying machines. He was always seeking the perfect balance between art and beauty in design. He was interested in the bodies of animals. He studied the inner structure of the human body. Da Vinci kept journals of his thoughts. They were written left-handed and in mirror writing. He did this so that his ideas could not be stolen by others. Leonardo was truly an amazing and unusual genius.

Check Your Understanding

1. Which of the following pieces of information would *not* be relevant to the passage?
   a. Leonardo experimented with new types of paints in some of his paintings.
   b. Leonardo's sculptures demonstrated a sense of harmony in life.
   c. Leonardo designed many machines that could not be made.
   d. Columbus sailed to America during Leonardo's lifetime.

2. Why would Leonardo write his papers left-handed and in mirror writing?
   a. He was left-handed.
   b. He only saw things as if in a mirror.
   c. He was secretive and distrusted others.
   d. both a and c

3. What is the author's purpose in writing the passage?
   a. to encourage the reader to become an artist
   b. to persuade the reader
   c. to inform the reader
   d. to make the reader laugh

4. From the context of the passage, which of the following means about the same as **dukes**?
   a. kings of nations
   b. elected national leaders
   c. city rulers who inherit their jobs
   d. presidents of small countries

/4

Name ____________________

Warm-Up 29

Mae Jemison

Mae Jemison is both a scientist and a medical doctor. She is the first African American woman to travel into space. As a child, Jemison decided to become a scientist. She grew up in Chicago. There, an uncle introduced her to science. She soon became very interested in the subject. She was fascinated by astronomy. She loved reading **science fiction** books, such as *A Wrinkle in Time*.

Jemison received a grant to Stanford University when she was sixteen. She enjoyed taking classes in art, dance, theater, and African American studies. She graduated with a degree in chemical engineering and Afro-American studies. One summer, she worked as a doctor's assistant in a camp for refugees. During this time, she studied to become a doctor at a medical college. She served as a doctor in the Peace Corps after she completed medical school. Jemison worked on several projects for a health institute. There, she tried to find new ways to treat infectious diseases.

Jemison was accepted into the NASA space program in 1987. She completed her astronaut training the next year. She made her space flight in 1992 as a mission specialist on the space shuttle crew. Later, she left NASA and taught at a college. She started programs to increase hands-on science teaching for children in the United States. She also worked on a science-camp program for children from other nations. Jemison is now focused on improving healthcare in Africa.

Check Your Understanding

1. Which of these occupations has Mae Jemison done?
   a. doctor
   b. astronaut
   c. teacher
   d. all of the above

2. From the context of the passage, what is the meaning of **science fiction**?
   a. true stories of adventures in space
   b. imaginary stories of science adventures
   c. research documents
   d. books written by aliens

3. Which word refers to "a person displaced from his or her home"?
   a. international
   b. scholarship
   c. refugee
   d. founded

4. Which of the following events happened third?
   a. Jemison worked as a doctor for the Peace Corps.
   b. Jemison received a grant from Stanford.
   c. Jemison decided to become a scientist.
   d. Jemison went to Stanford University.

/4

Warm-Up 30

Name ____________________

Willie Mays

In the 1950s and early 1960s, you could start a serious argument about who was the best player in baseball. Yankee fans tended to support Mickey Mantle as a power hitter and swift-running center fielder. Giants fans favored Willie Mays. From the time he entered the league at the age of twenty in 1951, Mays was a great player. He could hit with great power. He could also run the bases with style and great speed. He could catch just about anything hit in the direction of center field. Mantle was fast, but Mays was an artist with the glove.

"The Catch" was made in the first game of the 1954 World Series. It became the standard beside which all other great fielding efforts were compared. With the score tied in the eighth inning and a runner on first, Cleveland Indians' slugger Vic Wertz smashed a towering drive into the far reaches of right center field at the Polo Grounds. Mays took off at the crack of the bat with his long-legged, fluid, smooth stride. He made the catch with his back to the plate. He turned and fired a perfect strike to second base, forcing the runner back to first. The Giants won in ten innings and swept the series.

Mays played from 1951 to 1973 and hit 660 home runs. He became the all-time leader in outfield putouts. He made many more **sensational** catches and won twelve Gold Gloves in fielding. When asked if any particular catch was his greatest, he responded, "I don't compare 'em, I just catch 'em."

Check Your Understanding

1. From the context of the passage, what is the meaning of **sensational**?
   - a. incredible
   - b. slow-moving
   - c. hard to see
   - d. running
2. Who is quoted in the last line of the passage?
   - a. a sportswriter
   - b. a manager
   - c. Mickey Mantle
   - d. Willie Mays
3. Which of the following is an opinion and *not* a fact?
   - a. Willie Mays was the greatest baseball player.
   - b. Mays hit twenty-two extra-inning home runs.
   - c. Mays hit his first home run off pitcher Warren Spahn.
   - d. Mays was often called the "Say Hey Kid."
4. What is a fluid running style?
   - a. running in water
   - b. easy, smooth leg movement
   - c. very slow
   - d. hard to see

/4

Answer Key

Answer Key

Interesting Places and Events

Page 9 Wait Until 2061

1. a
2. c
3. b
4. d

Page 10 Around the World in Seventy-Two Days

1. b
2. a
3. b
4. c

Page 11 Antarctica

1. c
2. d
3. b
4. a

Page 12 The Taj Mahal

1. b
2. b
3. d
4. a

Page 13 Dinosaur Provincial Park

1. a
2. b
3. b
4. c

Page 14 Deer Cave, Malaysia

1. d
2. a
3. c
4. a

Page 15 Niagara Falls

1. d
2. c
3. c
4. d

Page 16 Krakatoa

1. d
2. a
3. b
4. b

Page 17 Mysterious Explosion in Russia

1. b
2. a
3. d
4. a

Page 18 July 4, 1826

1. b
2. d
3. a
4. c

Page 19 The Coastal Redwoods

1. b
2. d
3. d
4. a

Page 20 Ice Ages

1. b
2. a
3. c
4. d

Page 21 The Grand Canyon

1. d
2. b
3. a
4. b

Page 22 The Metropolitan Museum of Art

1. b
2. c
3. b
4. c

Page 23 The Lincoln Memorial

1. b
2. c
3. d
4. c

Page 24 The Washington Monument

1. c
2. d
3. d
4. a

Page 25 The Appalachian Mountains

1. c
2. d
3. c
4. c

Page 26 The Statue of Liberty

1. c
2. c
3. b
4. b

Page 27 Angkor Wat

1. d
2. a
3. c
4. b

Page 28 The Eiffel Tower

1. d
2. b
3. b
4. d

Page 29 The World Cup

1. d
2. d
3. a
4. d

Page 30 Mount Rushmore

1. c
2. d
3. c
4. a

Page 31 The Wall

1. b
2. d
3. c
4. c

Page 32 The Himalayas

1. c
2. b
3. d
4. c

Page 33 Ellis Island—Gateway to America

1. b
2. d
3. a
4. c

Page 34 The Iditarod Sled Dog Race

1. c
2. a
3. c
4. b

Page 35 The World Series

1. d
2. b
3. c
4. a

Page 36 The Golden Gate Bridge

1. a
2. b
3. c
4. b

Page 37 Daytona International Speedway

1. b
2. b
3. d
4. a

Page 38 Hoover Dam

1. c
2. b
3. d
4. b

Answer Key *(cont.)*

Scientifically Speaking

Page 41 Vermin of the Skies
1. a
2. b
3. d
4. c

Page 42 The Lost Planet
1. c
2. c
3. d
4. c

Page 43 Rain
1. c
2. c
3. b
4. a

Page 44 Decibel Levels
1. b
2. b
3. d
4. b

Page 45 Natural Chimneys
1. a
2. c
3. b
4. d

Page 46 Threats to Earth
1. b
2. d
3. c
4. d

Page 47 The First Professional Woman Astronomer
1. b
2. b
3. d
4. b

Page 48 Dangerous African Mammals
1. b
2. d
3. a
4. d

Page 49 You Wouldn't Want to Live on Venus
1. c
2. d
3. a
4. d

Page 50 The Heaviest Flying Bird
1. d
2. c
3. c
4. b

Page 51 Bioluminescence at Sea
1. c
2. d
3. d
4. c

Page 52 Lightning
1. d
2. d
3. d
4. a

Page 53 The Largest Volcano on Earth
1. c
2. b
3. d
4. a

Page 54 Jupiter—The Planetary Giant
1. b
2. d
3. a
4. c

Page 55 Tide Pools
1. b
2. b
3. a
4. b

Page 56 The Extinct Quagga
1. c
2. b
3. c
4. c

Page 57 The KT Event
1. d
2. d
3. d
4. a

Page 58 Animal Vision
1. a
2. a
3. b
4. c

Page 59 Mercury
1. b
2. a
3. b
4. d

Page 60 Animal Messages
1. c
2. b
3. d
4. d

Page 61 The Human Brain
1. a
2. c
3. a
4. d

Page 62 Snow
1. b
2. c
3. a
4. b

Page 63 Tornadoes
1. c
2. d
3. d
4. b

Page 64 The Laws of Motion
1. c
2. c
3. b
4. a

Page 65 Clouds
1. b
2. d
3. a
4. a

Page 66 Lions
1. b
2. c
3. b
4. b

Page 67 Water
1. b
2. d
3. b
4. d

Page 68 The Human Eye
1. a
2. b
3. a
4. c

Page 69 Goblin Sharks
1. c
2. c
3. b
4. c

Page 70 A Plant Larger Than a Whale
1. d
2. c
3. c
4. a

Answer Key *(cont.)*

From the Past

Page 73 She Was Dressed to Meet an Iceberg

1. c
2. a
3. c
4. b

Page 74 The Female Paul Revere

1. c
2. d
3. d
4. a

Page 75 He Loved His Mother

1. b
2. d
3. c
4. a

Page 76 The Rosetta Stone

1. a
2. c
3. a
4. a

Page 77 The Mausoleum of Halicarnassus

1. d
2. b
3. b
4. d

Page 78 The Invention of Basketball

1. c
2. b
3. c
4. d

Page 79 Laura Ingalls Wilder: Pioneer Author

1. a
2. b
3. d
4. c

Page 80 Food on the *Mayflower*

1. d
2. b
3. b
4. a

Page 81 The Library at Alexandria

1. d
2. d
3. b
4. a

Page 82 John Adams Defends British Soldiers

1. b
2. d
3. b
4. a

Page 83 The Travels of Marco Polo

1. a
2. d
3. c
4. b

Page 84 An Unusual Pharaoh

1. b
2. c
3. b
4. a

Page 85 A Number Challenge

1. d
2. d
3. d
4. c

Page 86 The History of the Book

1. d
2. b
3. c
4. c

Page 87 Female Pirates

1. b
2. b
3. b
4. c

Page 88 Kites

1. d
2. c
3. c
4. a

Page 89 Presidential Pets

1. b
2. d
3. a
4. d

Page 90 The Iceman

1. a
2. b
3. d
4. a

Page 91 Attempted Presidential Assassinations

1. d
2. b
3. d
4. a

Page 92 America's Forgotten Warriors

1. d
2. b
3. a
4. c

Page 93 The First Great Emperor

1. c
2. b
3. d
4. d

Page 94 Lincoln's Man

1. a
2. b
3. a
4. b

Page 95 The First Ferris Wheel

1. b
2. d
3. a
4. b

Page 96 Hatshepsut: The Lost Egyptian Queen

1. a
2. d
3. d
4. b

Page 97 The Ford Model T

1. d
2. c
3. d
4. d

Page 98 The Gibson Homer

1. d
2. b
3. a
4. a

Page 99 Homer Plessy Refuses to Give Up His Seat

1. b
2. a
3. d
4. d

Page 100 Old-Time Country Schools

1. d
2. d
3. b
4. b

Page 101 The Triangle Shirtwaist Factory Fire

1. b
2. b
3. c
4. d

Answer Key *(cont.)*

Page 102 Making Maple Syrup
1. d
2. c
3. a
4. c

Did You Know?

Page 105 Your Meniscus Is Leaking
1. c
2. a
3. c
4. d

Page 106 The Compass in Your Nose
1. c
2. b
3. b
4. c

Page 107 Snail Training
1. d
2. c
3. c
4. a

Page 108 Earthworm Pets
1. b
2. a
3. d
4. a

Page 109 The Invention of Silly Putty®
1. c
2. d
3. d
4. a

Page 110 Your Hair Is Dead
1. c
2. d
3. c
4. d

Page 111 How Big Is a Googol?
1. d
2. d
3. c
4. c

Page 112 Sharks Are Survivors
1. c
2. b
3. d
4. c

Page 113 LEGO® Bricks
1. a
2. b
3. d
4. c

Page 114 QWERTY
1. d
2. d
3. a
4. c

Page 115 Grizzly Bears
1. d
2. a
3. d
4. b

Page 116 Slinkity Slinkys®
1. b
2. b
3. a
4. d

Page 117 Keeping Toads and Frogs
1. c
2. c
3. b
4. d

Page 118 Save That Pencil
1. d
2. c
3. d
4. a

Page 119 The Safety Pin
1. d
2. a
3. d
4. d

Page 120 Count to One Billion
1. a
2. c
3. c
4. d

Page 121 Tsunamis
1. c
2. d
3. b
4. b

Page 122 Skunks
1. d
2. d
3. a
4. a

Page 123 The Latin in Your English
1. d
2. a
3. b
4. a

Page 124 Heartbeats
1. d
2. d
3. a
4. b

Page 125 Cricket-Jumping Contests
1. b
2. b
3. a
4. d

Page 126 The Liberty Bell
1. b
2. c
3. d
4. a

Page 127 "Big Mama" Oviraptor
1. c
2. d
3. d
4. c

Page 128 Birthday Odds
1. a
2. d
3. b
4. b

Page 129 Be a Better Speller
1. c
2. b
3. d
4. c

Page 130 Frozen Food
1. c
2. a
3. b
4. a

Page 131 Checkers
1. c
2. d
3. b
4. b

Page 132 Author Roald Dahl
1. b
2. c
3. a
4. d

Page 133 Making Crayons
1. d
2. a
3. d
4. c

Answer Key *(cont.)*

Page 134 American Idioms
1. c
2. b
3. a
4. b

Fascinating People

Page 137 Beverly Cleary
1. c
2. d
3. a
4. b

Page 138 He Mailed Himself to Freedom
1. d
2. b
3. a
4. b

Page 139 Hypatia
1. c
2. d
3. a
4. d

Page 140 The Secret Soldier
1. b
2. a
3. c
4. d

Page 141 The Most Important Woman in America
1. c
2. c
3. d
4. d

Page 142 Buffalo Bill Cody
1. a
2. c
3. b
4. d

Page 143 "Eureka! I've Found It!"
1. d
2. c
3. b
4. b

Page 144 First Emperor of the United States
1. a
2. d
3. b
4. c

Page 145 Steven Spielberg
1. d
2. a
3. c
4. c

Page 146 Galileo Galilei
1. b
2. d
3. d
4. a

Page 147 One-Eyed Charley
1. a
2. b
3. d
4. d

Page 148 The Librarian Who Measured Earth
1. b
2. d
3. c
4. a

Page 149 Sir Walter Raleigh
1. b
2. a
3. a
4. c

Page 150 The One-Armed Explorer
1. b
2. a
3. c
4. b

Page 151 Isaac Newton: Genius at Work
1. d
2. b
3. d
4. d

Page 152 Alexander the Great
1. a
2. a
3. d
4. b

Page 153 Sir Francis Drake
1. a
2. a
3. c
4. c

Page 154 Claude Monet
1. b
2. d
3. a
4. d

Page 155 Steve Jobs
1. b
2. a
3. a
4. d

Page 156 Oprah Winfrey
1. b
2. d
3. a
4. c

Page 157 Dizzy Dean
1. d
2. a
3. d
4. d

Page 158 Michael Jordan
1. c
2. b
3. a
4. d

Page 159 Eliza Harris
1. d
2. b
3. d
4. a

Page 160 Nelson Mandela
1. a
2. b
3. b
4. d

Page 161 Louis Braille
1. a
2. a
3. d
4. b

Page 162 Julius Caesar
1. c
2. b
3. a
4. d

Page 163 Bill Gates
1. c
2. a
3. b
4. b

Page 164 Leonardo Da Vinci
1. d
2. d
3. c
4. c

Page 165 Mae Jemison
1. d
2. b
3. c
4. d

Page 166 Willie Mays
1. a
2. d
3. a
4. b

Self-Monitoring Reading Strategies

Use these steps with your students so they can monitor their own reading comprehension. Be sure to go over each step with the class. Distribute a copy to each student or enlarge to make a class poster.

Step 1: Do I Understand?

Read a paragraph. Then ask, "Do I totally understand everything in this paragraph?" Use a pencil to mark a light **X** next to each paragraph that you comprehend and a light question mark next to each paragraph that contains anything you do not understand.

Step 2: What Have I Just Read?

At the end of each paragraph, stop and summarize silently to yourself, in your own words, what you have read. You may look back at the text during this activity.

Step 3: Does It Make Sense Now?

Finish reading the passage. Return to each paragraph that has a penciled question mark next to it and reread it. Does it make sense now? If so, great! If not, move on to step 4.

Step 4: Why Am I Having This Trouble?

Pinpoint the problem. Is the difficulty to do with unfamiliar words or concepts? Is the sentence structure too complex? Is it because you know little background information about the topic? It's important that you identify the specific stumbling block(s) before you move on to step 5.

Step 5: Where Can I Get Help?

Try a variety of aids to help you understand the text: the Internet, glossary, appendix, dictionary, thesaurus, encyclopedia, chapter summary, etc. Depending on what you are reading, use the resource(s) that will help you the most. If confusion remains after going through these five steps, ask a classmate or teacher for assistance.

As students become more comfortable with this strategy, you may want to make a rule that the students cannot ask for help from you unless they can do the following:

- identify the exact source of their confusion
- describe the steps they've already taken on their own to resolve the problem

Leveling Chart

Page #	Flesch-Kincaid Grade Level
Interesting Places and Events	
9	7.0
10	7.0
11	7.0
12	6.9
13	6.6
14	6.1
15	7.5*
16	6.7
17	6.3
18	7.7*
19	6.8
20	6.6
21	6.4
22	6.4
23	6.9
24	6.6
25	8.1*
26	6.8
27	6.5
28	7.0
29	6.5
30	8.2*
31	7.2*
32	6.9
33	6.8
34	6.2
35	7.0
36	7.0
37	7.0
38	6.9
Scientifically Speaking	
41	6.7
42	6.9
43	6.9
44	6.7
45	6.7
46	6.7
47	7.0
48	6.5
49	6.5
50	6.0
51	6.8
52	6.3
53	7.0
54	6.6
55	6.0
56	6.6
57	6.7
58	6.8
59	6.9
60	6.7
61	6.8
Scientifically Speaking *(cont.)*	
62	6.5
63	6.9
64	6.8
65	6.0
66	6.7
67	6.3
68	6.8
69	6.7
70	7.0
From the Past	
73	6.8
74	6.9
75	6.6
76	6.9
77	6.8
78	6.6
79	6.8
80	6.1
81	6.9
82	6.8
83	6.3
84	6.8
85	6.7
86	6.7
87	6.5
88	6.5
89	6.6
90	6.4
91	7.0
92	6.9
93	6.9
94	6.8
95	6.6
96	6.8
97	6.5
98	6.1
99	7.0
100	6.0
101	6.5
102	6.0
Did You Know?	
105	7.1*
106	6.6
107	6.1
108	6.0
109	6.3
110	6.7
111	6.9
112	6.4
113	6.4
114	6.4
115	6.9
Did You Know? *(cont.)*	
116	6.8
117	6.0
118	6.7
119	6.6
120	6.9
121	6.9
122	6.7
123	7.5*
124	6.2
125	6.2
126	7.3*
127	8.2*
128	7.0
129	6.0
130	6.6
131	6.5
132	6.7
133	6.8
134	6.8
Fascinating People	
137	6.6
138	6.5
139	6.4
140	6.6
141	6.9
142	7.0
143	6.9
144	6.7
145	6.9
146	6.7
147	6.7
148	7.0
149	6.3
150	6.9
151	6.6
152	6.6
153	6.8
154	6.7
155	6.5
156	6.8
157	6.8
158	6.1
159	6.7
160	6.9
161	6.0
162	6.5
163	6.6
164	6.6
165	7.4*
166	6.3

Tracking Sheet

Interesting Places and Events		Scientifically Speaking		From the Past		Did You Know?		Fascinating People	
Page 9		Page 41		Page 73		Page 105		Page 137	
Page 10		Page 42		Page 74		Page 106		Page 138	
Page 11		Page 43		Page 75		Page 107		Page 139	
Page 12		Page 44		Page 76		Page 108		Page 140	
Page 13		Page 45		Page 77		Page 109		Page 141	
Page 14		Page 46		Page 78		Page 110		Page 142	
Page 15		Page 47		Page 79		Page 111		Page 143	
Page 16		Page 48		Page 80		Page 112		Page 144	
Page 17		Page 49		Page 81		Page 113		Page 145	
Page 18		Page 50		Page 82		Page 114		Page 146	
Page 19		Page 51		Page 83		Page 115		Page 147	
Page 20		Page 52		Page 84		Page 116		Page 148	
Page 21		Page 53		Page 85		Page 117		Page 149	
Page 22		Page 54		Page 86		Page 118		Page 150	
Page 23		Page 55		Page 87		Page 119		Page 151	
Page 24		Page 56		Page 88		Page 120		Page 152	
Page 25		Page 57		Page 89		Page 121		Page 153	
Page 26		Page 58		Page 90		Page 122		Page 154	
Page 27		Page 59		Page 91		Page 123		Page 155	
Page 28		Page 60		Page 92		Page 124		Page 156	
Page 29		Page 61		Page 93		Page 125		Page 157	
Page 30		Page 62		Page 94		Page 126		Page 158	
Page 31		Page 63		Page 95		Page 127		Page 159	
Page 32		Page 64		Page 96		Page 128		Page 160	
Page 33		Page 65		Page 97		Page 129		Page 161	
Page 34		Page 66		Page 98		Page 130		Page 162	
Page 35		Page 67		Page 99		Page 131		Page 163	
Page 36		Page 68		Page 100		Page 132		Page 164	
Page 37		Page 69		Page 101		Page 133		Page 165	
Page 38		Page 70		Page 102		Page 134		Page 166	